CORAL REEF
COLLAPSE

By Carol Hand

ECOLOGICAL **DISASTERS**

Content Consultant

Richard B. Aronson
Professor of Biological Sciences
Florida Institute of Technology

Essential Library

An Imprint of Abdo Publishing | abdopublishing.com

abdopublishing.com

Published by Abdo Publishing, a division of ABDO, PO Box 398166, Minneapolis, Minnesota 55439. Copyright © 2018 by Abdo Consulting Group, Inc. International copyrights reserved in all countries. No part of this book may be reproduced in any form without written permission from the publisher. Essential Library™ is a trademark and logo of Abdo Publishing.

Printed in the United States of America, North Mankato, Minnesota
042017
092017

THIS BOOK CONTAINS
RECYCLED MATERIALS

Cover Photo: Rainer von Brandis/iStockphoto
Interior Photos: Debra James/Shutterstock Images, 4–5; JC Photo/Shutterstock Images, 6; NASA/GSFC/LaRC/JPL/MISR Team, 8; The Ocean Agency/XL Catlin Seaview Survey, 10, 43, 99 (middle); RNGS/RTR/Newscom, 12; Willyam Bradberry/Shutterstock Images, 14; Peter Visscher/Dorling Kindersley/Thinkstock, 16; NanoStockk/iStockphoto, 17; World Resources Institute, 18–19; G. P. Schmahl/NOAA FGBNMS Manager, 20; iStockphoto, 21, 29, 52, 55, 56–57, 64, 66, 72–73, 76–77, 79, 83, 84, 86–87, 96, 98 (left), 98 (bottom right), 99 (bottom); John A. Anderson/Shutterstock Images, 25; Durk Talsma/iStockphoto, 26–27, 98 (top right); Xuan Huongho/iStockphoto, 30; NG Images/Alamy, 32; Charles D. Winters/Science Source, 33, 98 (middle right); National Oceanic and Atmospheric Administration, 35; Rainer von Brandis/iStockphoto, 36, 40, 44–45, 89, 93, 99 (top); Keith A. Ellenbogen/AP Images, 38–39; Inna Bigun/Shutterstock Images, 47; Nature Picture Library/Alamy, 48–49; Shutterstock Images, 50, 74; R. B. Aronson, 59, 91; Suzanne Long/Alamy, 60; Michael Patrick O'Neill/Science Source, 62; Ramdan Nain/iStockphoto, 68; Sijori Images/Barcroft India/Barcroft Media/Getty Images, 71; NOAA, 80; Jay Directo/AFP/Getty Images, 95

Editor: Melissa York
Series Designer: Laura Polzin

Publisher's Cataloging-in-Publication Data

Names: Hand, Carol, author.
Title: Coral reef collapse / by Carol Hand.
Description: Minneapolis, MN : Abdo Publishing, 2018. | Series: Ecological
    disasters | Includes bibliographical references and index.
Identifiers: LCCN 2016962131 | ISBN 9781532110214 (lib. bdg.) |
    ISBN 9781680788068 (ebook)
Subjects: LCSH: Coral reef ecology--Juvenile literature. | Environmental
    degradation--Juvenile literature. | Ecological disturbances--Juvenile literature.
Classification: DDC 577.7--dc23
LC record available at http://lccn.loc.gov/2016962131

CONTENTS

Chapter ONE

THE GREAT BARRIER REEF

G littering coral reefs dot the shallow tropical oceans, forming a broken necklace around Earth's equator. Diving down into the reefs, visitors are surrounded by thousands of rainbow-colored fish darting among a forest of coral heads and branches. They see the waving tentacles of corals and anemones, with shy eels and octopi peeking out among the branches. They see sea slugs and crabs crawling over the

Many species of coral, fish, and other organisms make up the ecosystem of the Great Barrier Reef off the coast of Australia.

Coral structures that are a part of the Great Barrier Reef can be seen above the water.

reef surfaces. The largest jewel in this necklace of teeming underwater cities is Australia's Great Barrier Reef. Roughly the size of Germany, or half as big as Texas, the Great Barrier Reef (GBR) can be easily seen from space. The GBR is the world's largest barrier reef and the world's largest living structure. It stretches along the northeastern coast of the Australian state of Queensland, reaching 1,400 miles (2,300 km) from north of Cape York peninsula down south almost to Brisbane. The Great Barrier Reef Marine Park, which contains and protects the GBR, is between 40 and 155 miles (60 and 250 km) wide and covers an area of nearly 133,000 square miles (344,000 sq km). Its treasures include approximately 3,000 individual reefs and more than 1,000 islands.[1]

The GBR is not only a region of unsurpassed beauty; it is also essential to Australia's life and economy. The Australian government protects and manages the GBR through the Great Barrier Reef Marine Park Authority. The reef is zoned to allow different sustainable human activities, including tourism, fishing, boating, and commercial shipping, in different areas of the park. Tourism, commercial fishing, and recreational fishing on and around the reef add $6.9 billion (in Australian dollars) to the Australian economy every year.[2] These industries support approximately 70,000 jobs.[3] But this vibrant community is dying. Many scientists think it is already doomed.

The Great Barrier Reef Marine Park, which contains and protects the Great Barrier Reef, is the size of 70 million football fields.[4]

BIODIVERSITY OF THE GBR

From the air, one can see the jagged structures of the GBR curve around the coast of Australia, lighter in color than the surrounding water. Occasional islands break the surface. The structures are masses of hard corals, plus sponges and other organisms. The corals produce their own hard skeletons of calcium carbonate, or limestone. The reef has more than 600 species of corals. Some are reef-building hard corals. Others are soft corals, such as sea fans. Living coral polyps contain single-celled algae. The algae use photosynthesis to provide themselves and the polyps with energy. These symbiotic algae, plus the reef's free-living algae, support the ecosystem's food web. In deeper waters where the sun can't reach, hard corals cannot build massive reef frameworks, but near shore, sunlight and therefore reefs extend down to an average depth of 115 feet (35 m). The reefs support an ecosystem of amazing complexity.

THE GBR FROM SPACE

Reefs along the GBR reach upward from the shallow seafloor. The skeletons within the reefs are interconnected by their calcium carbonate structures. Corals form most of the reef, but trillions of tiny, pink coralline algae also secrete calcium carbonate and help cement the reef together. This true-color image of the GBR, taken by NASA's Terra satellite on August 26, 2000, shows part of the central portion of the reef near the Queensland coast.

Living among the sessile, or attached, corals are more than 100 species of jellyfish; 3,000 species of mollusks; 500 species of worms; 1,625 species of fish, including 133 types of sharks and rays; and more than 30 species of dolphins and whales.[5] Six of the world's seven sea turtle species visit the GBR. Raine Island in the GBR is the world's largest breeding site for green turtles. At least 242 bird species visit the GBR, many of them breeding on the cays and islands.[6] The teeming, brightly colored life of the coral reef is more diverse than any ecosystem on Earth except the tropical rain forest. But the Great Barrier Reef is changing rapidly.

THE GBR AND CLIMATE CHANGE

The major threat to the Great Barrier Reef is climate change, a complex process with multiple effects. Two effects are especially dangerous to the reef: rising temperatures and increasing acidity in the ocean. The most visible impact is coral bleaching, or whitening, caused by high temperatures, which puts stress on corals. Temperature-stressed corals expel their zooxanthellae, the tiny algae that live inside their tissues. Zooxanthellae keep the corals alive: their photosynthesis produces most of the corals' food. Corals can recover from short periods of increased temperatures, but if the heat continues, they die. An increase of only

1.8 to 2.7 degrees Fahrenheit (1.0 to 1.5°C) for six weeks results in extensive coral bleaching, followed by death unless reef temperatures quickly return to normal.[7]

Since 1979, the GBR has experienced eight mass bleaching events as a result of increasing temperatures. Two very bad years were 1998 and 2002. During those two years, 42 and 54 percent of the reefs, respectively, were bleached. Then, during the years 2015–2016, the most extreme bleaching event ever recorded on the GBR occurred. Researchers reported that 93 percent of the reefs, especially those in the northern region, suffered from some level of bleaching.[8] All of these bleaching events were associated with an El Niño event, a periodic weather pattern that brings warmer-than-average water to the Pacific Ocean. When combined with global warming, El Niño events result in major bleaching during that year or the next. The 1997–1998 El Niño was the strongest in recorded history, and the 2015–2016 event was a close second. The 2002 weather pattern was moderately strong.

If the water cools sufficiently, reefs may rebound, but many corals—especially old, slow-growing ones—take decades to recover. In early 2016, divers near Cape York, at the reef's northeastern tip, discovered that half of the corals had already died, and a full 75 percent in the reef's northern half were damaged.[9] Over the hot, still summer, the reefs

WHAT IS BIODIVERSITY?

Biodiversity, or biological diversity, refers to the variety of living organisms in an ecosystem. Biodiversity encompasses variety in the species present, the genes they contain, and the ecosystems they live in. The GBR is biodiverse in all of these ways. Biodiversity is essential ecologically because it helps stabilize an ecosystem. Biodiverse ecosystems are productive, healthy, self-sufficient, and better able to overcome disasters. If part of an ecosystem sickens or dies, high biodiversity allows the rest to survive and restore the system.

DOCUMENTING DEATH

Diver Richard Vevers was most disturbed by the smell. "When we got . . . back on the boat, we realized we just stank, stank of the smell of rotting animals." Vevers is chief executive of the Ocean Agency, an organization he founded to bring attention to environmental problems. He photographed Lizard Island reef, which was affected by the 2016 GBR bleaching event. He took pictures of the reef before bleaching began, just after bleaching started, and finally, weeks later, when its effects became obvious. The healthy reef was luxuriant with life. The dying reef was brilliant white—deceptively beautiful. But, several weeks later, Vevers said, "It was one of the most disgusting sights I've ever seen."[10] Hard corals were blanketed by algae and seaweed. Soft corals were decomposing, their flesh dripping off the reef structure. Other animals had disappeared. The reef was no longer diverse and colorful. Its corals were all dead.

were bathed in extremely warm water for months. This area of the reef had been considered its most pristine, and the 2016 bleaching event was the worst ever recorded at the site. Most of the southern reefs remained largely intact, due to heavy rain and cloud cover during the summer.

Climate change damage does not stop with bleaching. Climate change results primarily from fossil fuel burning, which raises temperatures in the atmosphere by releasing greenhouse gases. The most plentiful greenhouse gas in the atmosphere is carbon dioxide (CO_2). When carbon dioxide dissolves in the ocean, it reacts with water to become carbonic acid, which makes water more acidic. Corals are affected by acidification because of their calcium carbonate skeletons. Already existing coral skeletons may be corroded by the acid. The new coral growth may be slowed, resulting in weaker reefs that are more likely to erode. Recent studies show that some coral species may be able to control their internal acidity and cope with increasing levels of acid in the water. But studies indicate future acidification may damage the GBR.

OTHER IMPACTS

The GBR is threatened by more than climate change. It is damaged by shore-based pollution, including toxic chemicals from industry and nutrient runoff from agriculture and sewage. Excess nutrients speed up algal growth, blocking sunlight and causing algae to overgrow the reefs. In addition, some people cause direct damage to reefs. They drop anchors or carry out dredging and trawling, breaking off pieces of the reef structure. They use unsustainable and destructive fishing methods.

"The single biggest thing we can do to protect the Reef for the future is to greatly reduce greenhouse gas emissions as soon as possible."[11]

—*David Wachenfeld, director of reef recovery at the Great Barrier Reef Marine Park Authority*

Finally, similar to marine organisms throughout the oceans, residents of the GBR are succumbing to plastic pollution. Polyps are filter feeders. They draw into their bodies whatever is present in the water passing over them. This includes microplastics—tiny beads of plastic ground down by waves until they are small enough to become coral food. But corals cannot break down plastic, which remains in their digestive systems and may prevent them from digesting real food. When corals eat microplastics, they can starve.

THE FUTURE OF THE GBR

Research released in 2016 suggests the GBR may be in even more danger from climate change than previously suspected. Temperature spikes are known to kill corals, but temperature changes are not uniform across the reef. When part of the reef receives a

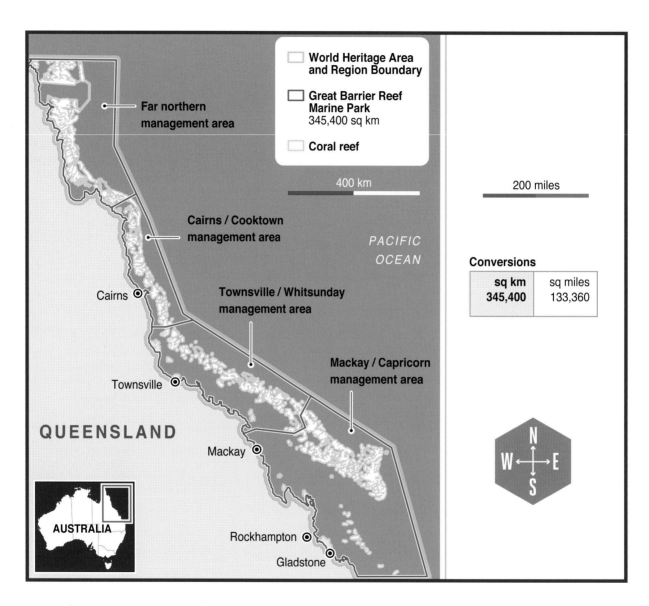

World Heritage Area and Region Boundary

Great Barrier Reef Marine Park 345,400 sq km

Coral reef

400 km

200 miles

PACIFIC OCEAN

Far northern management area

Cairns / Cooktown management area

Townsville / Whitsunday management area

Mackay / Capricorn management area

Cairns

Townsville

QUEENSLAND

Mackay

Rockhampton

Gladstone

AUSTRALIA

Conversions

sq km	sq miles
345,400	133,360

N W E S

Australia's Great Barrier Reef

pulse of warmth—a surge of gently warmed water—a few days before a temperature spike, this short time of adjustment prepares the reef and makes it more able to survive the temperature spike. But as temperatures rise, those pre-spike pulses will stop. Simultaneously, single temperature spikes will increase dramatically. These changes will occur within the next 40 years, and unless greenhouse gas emissions are drastically reduced, by the 2050s, the corals could die from bleaching.

Stress from climate change, plus stresses from pollution and other human actions, are combining to make the future of the GBR precarious at best. And what is happening to the GBR is happening to reefs around the world—not only rising temperatures and acidity, but also plastics pollution, overfishing, and damage due to runoff, construction, and vandalism. The devastation is rapid. Why are people letting this happen? What can be done about it?

Sea turtles are one of the many
organisms that populate a coral reef.

Chapter

TWO

WHAT IS A CORAL REEF?

In warm, shallow ocean water surrounding continents and islands, the skeletons of both living and dead corals form mounds or ridges. Skeletons of calcareous (calcium-containing) algae, mollusks, and other marine creatures add complex shapes. These hard, jagged structures are coral reefs. They vary in shape and size, depending on location and species. New, living coral polyps attach to the older structure. Eventually some structures breach the ocean's surface, becoming small coral islands, or cays. Underwater, the intricate coral architecture forms many hiding places. The reef provides food and shelter for thousands of species of fish and invertebrates, making reefs the most biodiverse marine habitat. Many tropical waters have few nutrients because the warm surface waters prevent deeper, nutrient-rich water from welling up. They are often considered marine deserts.

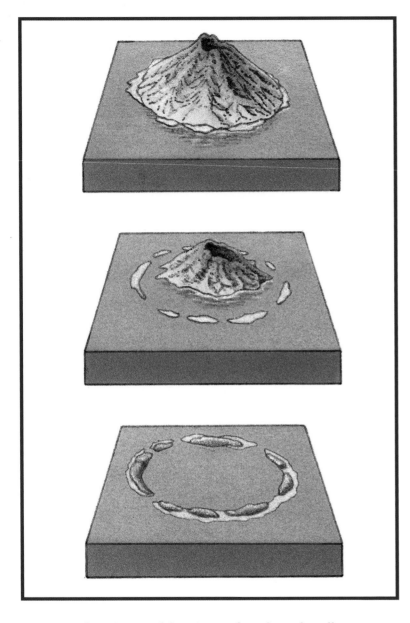

From top, **fringing reef, barrier reef, and coral atoll**

Coral reefs, with their ability to recycle and concentrate nutrients, form oases in those deserts.

The US National Ocean Service recognizes three distinct types of coral reefs. Fringing reefs surround and are connected to the edges of continents. They grow outward from the shore toward the sea and are the most common type of reef. Barrier reefs also follow and connect to shorelines, but they are separated from the shore by an expanse of open water, such as a deep lagoon. In the Pacific Ocean, a reef often forms a circle or oval around a sunken volcanic island with a saltwater lagoon in the center. This is a coral atoll.

REEFS AROUND THE WORLD

Coral reefs can only live under specific conditions, which limits their locations on Earth. They need sunlight, because they

depend for food on algae that live inside the coral tissues. These algae photosynthesize, so the water must be shallow and clear enough for light to penetrate. Most corals live in water no deeper than 165 feet (50 m). The water must be clear and warm, from 68 to 90 degrees Fahrenheit (20 to 32° C). Thus, corals occur either in tropical waters or in waters where tropical currents flow past. Finally, they require water with a high salt content, so they are not found in estuaries, where rivers drain freshwater into the ocean.

These unique conditions are found offshore in more than 100 countries around the world. Reefs lie between the Tropics of Cancer and Capricorn, the two lines of latitude that form the boundary of the tropics. They occur in the Pacific and Indian Oceans, the Caribbean and Red Seas, and the Persian Gulf. The Atlantic Ocean has just a few, and a few are also found in subtropical areas where warm currents flow, such as near southern Japan. According to the World Atlas of Coral Reefs, prepared by the United Nations Environment Programme, there are an estimated 110,000 square miles (284,000 sq km) of coral reefs around the world.[1]

CORAL ATOLL FORMATION
The formation of a coral atoll in the Pacific Ocean shows all three major types of reefs. When the volcano is actively depositing lava, the island grows. Corals attach around its edge, forming a fringing reef. As the volcano becomes inactive, the island begins sinking. Eventually a lagoon forms between the island and the reef, turning the fringing reef into a barrier reef. Finally, the volcanic island subsides completely and its central crater fills with seawater, forming a lagoon. The lagoon, surrounded by a ring of growing coral, forms an atoll. The entire process may take 30 million years.

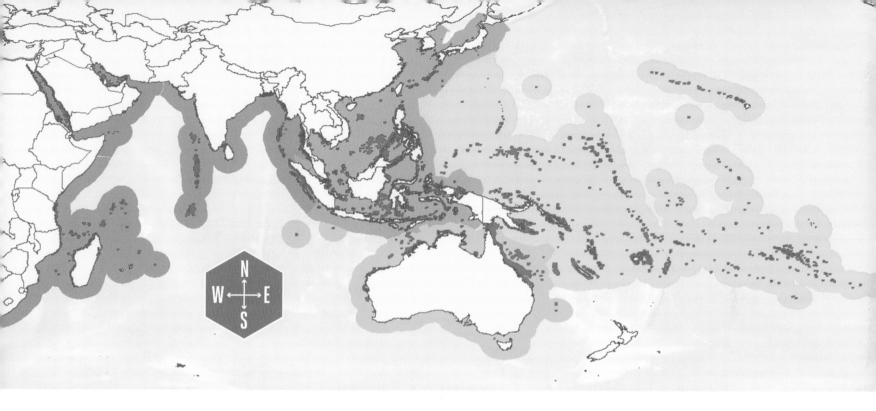

CORALS AND THEIR ZOOXANTHELLAE

Corals are invertebrate animals, members of phylum Cnidaria. Cnidarians' most unusual features are stinging cells called cnidoblasts. Within each cnidoblast is a nematocyst, a capsule containing a thread-like, coiled, hollow tube with toxic barbs. The tube is ejected to sting passing prey or enemies. Otherwise, cnidarians are extremely diverse, including jellyfish, corals, and sea anemones. Corals themselves are divided into two major groups: hard corals and soft corals. The soft coral group includes flexible sea whips and sea fans. Their skeletons are mostly made of protein. Hard corals are reef builders, and their rigid skeletons are made of calcium carbonate. The living portion of a coral is a colony of delicate, tentacled polyps that forms a thin sheet over the nonliving skeleton.

CORAL REEFS

ATLANTIC

AUSTRALIA

INDIAN OCEAN

MIDDLE EAST

PACIFIC

SOUTHEAST ASIA

Reefs do not do well in areas with rich nutrients, such as the upwelling zones off the west coasts of Africa and South America.

Corals are considered foundation species. The solid architecture of the coral reef and the nutrients it concentrates maintain a highly diverse ecosystem. Without the foundation species, other organisms would lose their habitat and food sources, and the ecosystem would collapse. Foundation species such as corals, which drastically change the environment around them, are also called ecosystem engineers.

Each coral polyp partners with tiny, single-celled algae called zooxanthellae. Their relationship is mutualistic—it benefits both partners. Zooxanthellae live within the tissues of the coral polyps, which give them a safe place to grow. They

"Reefs are often compared to rainforests, which are the only other ecosystem that can boast anywhere near the amount of biodiversity found on a reef. Coral reefs are sometimes called rainforests of the seas."[2]

—*National Oceanic and Atmospheric Administration (NOAA) Fisheries*

THE CORAL POLYP

A single coral polyp resembles a tiny sea anemone, with a cylindrical body and a mouth on top surrounded by a ring of tentacles. These tiny, fragile animals, no more than 0.25 to 12 inches (0.64 to 30.5 cm) across, can build structures spanning more than 1,000 miles (1,600 km). Polyps receive up to 90 percent or more of the massive energy required for this feat from their zooxanthellae.[3] They are also predators. The nematocysts located along their tentacles act like tiny harpoons. When a zooplankton, such as a tiny crustacean, brushes past a tentacle, it triggers a nematocyst. The nematocyst fires, hitting the crustacean with a dart that delivers a toxin. The polyp uses its tentacles to sweep the paralyzed prey into its mouth. Coral polyps also trap tiny bacteria in the mucus that covers their bodies. They use cilia—tiny, hairlike structures on the tentacles—to sweep the trapped bacteria into their mouths.

obtain chemicals needed for photosynthesis from the coral animals' waste from digesting protein. The zooxanthellae can give the coral most of the products of their photosynthesis, including oxygen, glucose, and glycerol. Corals obtain most of their amino acids from their zooplankton prey. The coral uses these products to grow, making fats, proteins, carbohydrates, and calcium carbonate. This strong mutualism results in a tight recycling of nutrients in the coral reef, making the reef much more productive than its surrounding, nutrient-poor waters. Zooxanthellae are also responsible for the corals' bright colors. The limestone skeleton is white, and coral polyps are transparent. But each square centimeter of coral tissue contains several million zooxanthellae cells, all of which produce pigments that lend their colors to the corals. Corals and zooxanthellae work together to make some pigments, with the algae beginning the chemical reactions and the corals finishing the process.

INTERACTING ECOSYSTEMS

Coral reefs are connected to other ecosystems, especially to highly productive seagrass beds and coastal mangrove forests. These three ecosystems are often found together, and fish and

Mangrove trees grow in warm saltwater in the tropics worldwide.

other animals move seamlessly through all of them. The gray snapper fish, for example, depends on all three ecosystems during different parts of its life cycle.

DEEP-WATER CORALS

Corals are not just warm-water, light-loving species. In the past two decades, scientists have discovered almost as many coral species living in cold water and dim light, or even darkness, at depths down to 20,000 feet (6,000 m). Instead of depending on zooxanthellae, deep-sea corals obtain their energy and nutrients by trapping zooplankton from passing currents. Deep-sea corals are widely distributed in ocean basins around the world, living in water as cold as 30 degrees Fahrenheit (-1°C). Some deep-sea coral colonies are extremely old—one black coral colony off Hawaii is 4,265 years old.[4] Just as shallow-water corals do, these deep-water foundation species provide the basis for highly diverse ecosystems.

Seagrasses are flowering plants, related to grasses and lilies. Vast underwater seagrass meadows provide food and hiding places for many sea-dwelling grazers. Similar to corals, seagrasses live in shallow waters near shore, where light for photosynthesis reaches the bottom. Mangrove forests are onshore ecosystems. Their mangrove tree species live with their roots in saltwater. Many species of birds, insects, reptiles and amphibians live in and around the mangrove trees. The trees' partially submerged roots support ocean organisms including barnacles, oysters, crabs, sponges, and anemones.

These three ecosystems and their interactions make coastal tropical oceans some of the most profoundly rich and exciting regions on Earth. Decomposing mangrove leaves and wood provide nutrients that wash over seagrass beds and coral reefs. But mangroves and seagrass beds also filter out extra nutrients before they reach the reefs. Reefs protect seagrasses and mangroves from erosion caused by storm waves. Mangrove roots and seagrasses provide protected habitats for young fish that will populate coral reefs. This mutual protection is a major reason these three ecosystems occur together.

Coral reefs are complex, varied, and extremely important to the tropical coastal environment. These busy, natural underwater cities support and maintain thousands of marine species. They also provide constant and essential ecosystem services to humans. They provide nurseries for young fish and are a major food source for nearby communities. Reefs are a key source of compounds used in medicines, including cancer treatments. They act as natural barriers, slowing coastal storms such as hurricanes. And they generate tourist dollars. According to a 2009 study, coral reefs provide an estimated $172 billion per year in ecosystem services—many of which people are not even aware are happening.[5]

"Coral reefs teem with life, covering less than one percent of the ocean floor, but supporting about 25 percent of all marine creatures."[6]

—National Geographic

SCIENCE CONNECTION
BUILDING A CORAL REEF

Reef-building corals usually form huge colonies. Corals release masses of eggs and sperm into the water at the same time. Some develop into free-floating larvae, or planulae. Eventually, the planulae that survive settle to the bottom and attach to hard surfaces such as rocks or coral skeletons. There, the planulae metamorphose into polyps. The settled polyps then bud, making hundreds or thousands of clones of themselves. Using materials from seawater, each polyp builds a hard, cup-shaped protective limestone skeleton around its base. The individual skeletons are connected to each other, forming the colony. Depending on the species, a single polyp can live from two years to hundreds of years, and a colony from five years to several centuries. One gigantic coral head on the GBR is approximately 1,200 years old.[7]

Hard corals are not the only reef builders. Crustose coralline algae (CCA) produce a hard, calcium-based crust that coats the coral structure and helps hold it together. Without CCA, the reef would be much weaker. The reef is also cemented together by sediment that fills the pores in the calcium structure, and by a limestone cement that precipitates from the seawater.

Year by year, corals add to their skeletons, building upward into the sunlit zone. A growing reef must build skeleton faster than the reef erodes. Massive boulder-shaped corals grow very slowly, between 0.2 and 1 inch (5 and 25 mm) per year. Branching corals, such as staghorns, grow more rapidly, up to 8 inches (20 cm) per year. Most of today's established coral reefs are between 5,000 and 10,000 years old.[8]

Boulder-shaped brain corals of the Caribbean grow slowly and anchor their reef systems.

THREE

HOW ARE OCEANS CHANGING?

The damaging effects of human activity on global climate started when people first began burning fossil fuels. These effects have greatly accelerated since the mid-1900s. Current levels of carbon dioxide in the atmosphere are the highest in 15 million years.[1] Higher levels of carbon dioxide and other greenhouse gases cause global temperatures to rise, leading to changes that include melting snow and ice,

Melting glaciers and sea ice contribute to sea level rise.

sea level rise, extreme heat events, and storms that are more frequent and more intense. Almost every system on Earth is tied to climate. Food and water supplies, the health of organisms and ecosystems, and of course the health of the oceans, are all at risk as climate change accelerates.

GREENHOUSE GASES

Greenhouse gases in the atmosphere trap infrared radiation, or heat. This causes the greenhouse effect, which keeps Earth warm enough to support life. Major greenhouse gases include carbon dioxide, methane, and nitrous oxide. All are present in tiny amounts; for example, the current proportion of carbon dioxide in the atmosphere is 0.04 percent. This level is much higher than at any time in the past 400,000 years.[3] In the short term, plants remove some carbon dioxide entering the atmosphere for photosynthesis. Eventually, greenhouse gases are absorbed by oceans and sediments, but absorption cannot keep up with the gases released by fossil fuel burning. As excess greenhouse gases (especially carbon dioxide) trap more heat, global temperatures rise.

Oceans make up approximately 70 percent of Earth's surface and hold nearly 97 percent of its water. Given the current rise in atmospheric greenhouse gases, it helps that so much of Earth's surface is covered with oceans. Oceans warm much more slowly than air, absorbing a tremendous amount of heat before they begin changing temperature. Thus, oceans are vital in absorbing excess heat and slowing the warming of the atmosphere. Since 1955, oceans have absorbed more than 90 percent of Earth's extra heat.[2] But even oceans have their limits, and ocean temperatures are beginning to rise.

SEA SURFACE TEMPERATURE

Rising ocean temperatures profoundly affect both oceans and land. Sea surface temperatures and sea levels are both rising. This affects coasts by increasing storms and floods. Ocean temperatures increase first and most rapidly at the surface, where sunlight hits the water. As the ocean surface warms, the water becomes less dense, changing the paths of ocean currents. Higher surface temperatures cause more evaporation, which increases rain and snow. More water vapor in the atmosphere also leads to stronger tropical storms and hurricanes.

Rising sea surface temperatures probably affect corals more than any other marine organism, but corals are not the only organisms stressed. High temperatures kill some organisms and affect the breeding and migration patterns of others. Critically, high temperatures slow the reproduction of krill, a tiny crustacean near the base of many marine food chains.

SEA LEVEL RISE

Two main factors cause sea level rise. The first is the melting of ice stored in glaciers and ice sheets on land or at sea. If a glacier or ice sheet loses more ice in summer than it gains in winter, its mass shrinks, and the melted water runs into the ocean. Second, as water warms, it expands a little.

Krill provide the main food for several types of penguins and whales, as well as many fish.

Sandbags fail to keep the rising sea from eroding the beach near a seaside restaurant in Hoi An, Vietnam.

The same amount of water takes up more space. This expansion raises sea level over all of Earth's oceans.

Scientists had predicted that, during this century, global sea levels would rise on average by more than two feet (0.6 m).[4] But a study released in March 2016 nearly doubles this estimate. The study also predicts that, if greenhouse gas emissions continue at present rates, oceans could rise more than six feet (2 m) by 2100.[5] These predictions are averages for the world ocean. Sea level rise varies greatly by location, depending on local geography and ocean currents. Rising sea levels will have their greatest impact on nearshore marine ecosystems, such as coral reefs, which depend on sunlight. As sea levels rise, these ecosystems will be deeper underwater, reducing the amount of light reaching the zooxanthellae and thereby slowing coral growth.

> "If the same amount of heat that has been buried in the upper 2 km [1.2 miles] of the ocean had gone into the atmosphere, the surface of the Earth would have warmed by a devastating 36°C [64.8 degrees Fahrenheit], rather than 1°C [1.8 degrees Fahrenheit], over the past century."[7]
>
> —Journalist Oliver Milman, paraphrasing 2016 IUCN report on ocean climate change

CARBON DIOXIDE AND RISING OCEAN ACIDITY

In the past 250 years, oceans have absorbed approximately 28 percent of the carbon dioxide produced by fossil fuel burning.[6] This might seem like a good thing, since this absorption removes carbon dioxide from the atmosphere and thereby slows temperature rise. But when carbon dioxide reacts with seawater, it forms carbonic acid. Adding acid to the water, or lowering its pH level, seriously stresses or kills ocean organisms. Increasing acidity is particularly damaging to corals and other organisms that build skeletons or shells

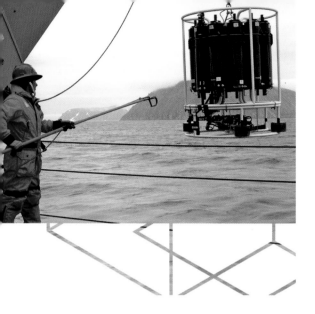

of calcium carbonate, because acid dissolves the mineral. Ultimately, rising acidity can destroy whole ecosystems, including coral reefs. It can also affect fish populations and the people who depend on them.

Changes in pH occur over many decades, but there are also short-term fluctuations. Increasing sea surface temperatures decrease the ocean's ability to absorb carbon dioxide. Warmer liquids hold less gas than cooler liquids. For example, heating a soda will make it go flat. Normally, winds mix surface water with deeper layers, bringing cool water to the surface. But as the surface warms, this mixing is less effective. The warm water remains in a layer on top, becomes saturated with carbon dioxide, and releases the excess carbon dioxide back into the atmosphere, adding to higher air temperatures. Patterns of carbon dioxide uptake and pH change vary throughout the oceans, and they are difficult to measure and predict.

OTHER OCEAN CHANGES

While the ocean is undergoing major shifts due to climate change, other serious problems are devastating marine ecosystems, including coral reefs. Eighty percent of these problems come from human activities on land.[9] These include oil spills and oil draining down rivers from homes and industries. Sediments, fertilizer runoff, sewage, and toxic pollutants run off the land and enter rivers and oceans. Plastic waste forms massive rotating pools of garbage in the oceans. Plastics kill and maim marine organisms of all kinds.

When these already existing marine hazards combine with the growing hazards of climate change, the ocean's future looks bleak. Prospects look particularly bad for coral reefs. Corals and many other tropical organisms already live near the edge of their temperature and pH ranges. Only a slight rise in heat or acidity can push them over the edge.

A laboratory experiment shows how coral dissolves when submerged in strong acid, a fast-motion version of the much slower reaction in nature.

THE PHYSICS OF OCEAN TEMPERATURES

Besides water's extremely high ability to absorb heat, other factors affect how ocean water handles temperature increases. The most important are depth, density, and salinity.

The ocean has three temperature zones. The surface layer, where sunlight strikes, is the warmest. Its average temperature varies with latitude, from 96.8 degrees Fahrenheit (36°C) at the equator to 28.4 degrees Fahrenheit (-2°C) at the poles. Water and heat in this layer mix thoroughly.

Below the surface layer is the thermocline, where temperature changes rapidly with water depth. In temperate zones, how deep the ocean thermocline reaches changes with the seasons. Its depth is stable in the tropics, where temperatures are warm all year. In polar regions, there is almost no thermocline. The ocean is cold from top to bottom.

The thermocline separates the surface layer from the third layer, the deep ocean, which contains 90 percent of the ocean's volume. The deep ocean is not mixed well. It contains horizontal layers of different densities and remains extremely cold, between 32 and 37.5 degrees Fahrenheit (0 to 3°C).

As salinity increases, water density increases. Freshwater entering oceans from rivers or melting glaciers dilutes salt and decreases water density. Evaporation increases it. When ice forms, salt remains in the water, making it denser. Variations in temperature, salinity, and density help water mix. Cold, dense water sinks. This movement drives a circulation pattern that moves water and heat around the world ocean. This vast ocean conveyor belt strongly affects world climate.

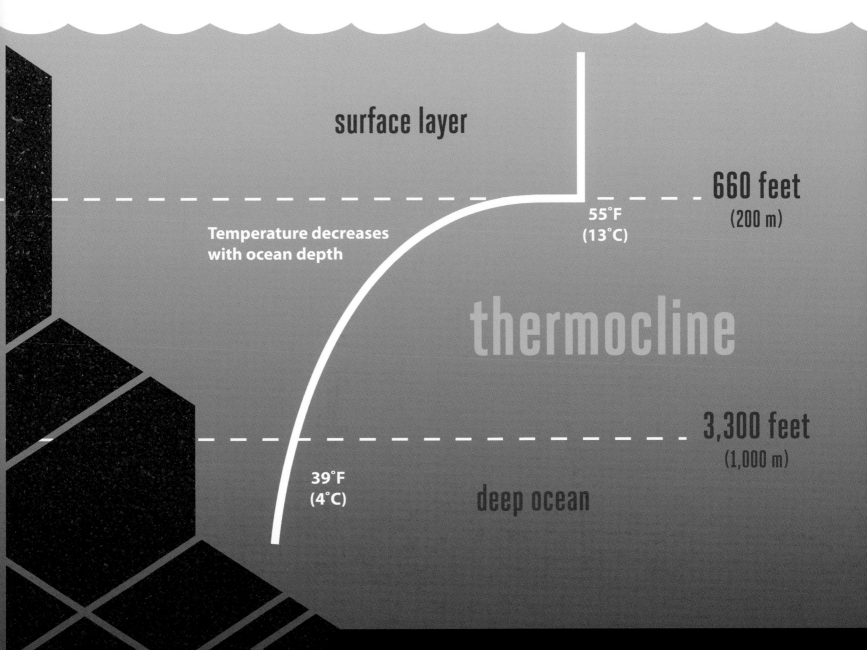

surface layer

660 feet
(200 m)

55°F
(13°C)

Temperature decreases
with ocean depth

thermocline

3,300 feet
(1,000 m)

39°F
(4°C)

deep ocean

The zones of the ocean

A researcher measures a bleached coral in the Seychelles in the Indian Ocean.

Chapter

FOUR

HOW DO RISING TEMPERATURES AFFECT CORAL REEFS?

Coral reefs are dying. Approximately 30 percent of the world's reefs have been destroyed in the last several decades. Another 30 to 50 percent may be destroyed by about 2025. In the Caribbean, coral cover has been reduced by 80 percent since the 1970s.[1] Destruction of reefs does not mean extinction of coral species. It means the death of most or all coral colonies in a given region, many of

"These bleaching events are coming more quickly, they are more severe and there are a number of coral reefs around the world that just are not being given enough time to truly recover between events."[3]

—*Mark Eakin, NOAA coral reef expert*

them hundreds or thousands of years old. El Niño weather events, which cause increases in Pacific Ocean temperatures, have had profound worldwide effects. Coral bleaching during the 1982–1983 El Niño killed more than 95 percent of Galapagos corals. The 1997–1998 El Niño was so strong it killed 16 percent of all corals on Earth.[2] Recently, rises in ocean temperature have caused bleaching events even in non–El Niño years. In 2005, a huge mass-bleaching event occurred in the Caribbean.

The drastic deaths of corals coincide with rising ocean temperatures. Records of ocean temperatures began in 1870. They show an

The whitened polyps on this branching hard coral have lost their zooxanthellae.

THE REEFS OF KIRITIMATI

Kiritimati, or Christmas Island, is a coral atoll in the tiny country of Kiribati in the Pacific Ocean 1,000 miles (1,600 km) south of Hawaii. Julia Baum of the University of Victoria in British Columbia visited the atoll in March 2016 with her colleague Kim Cobb of Georgia Tech. Kiritimati reef was affected by the 2015–2016 El Niño event, which raised temperatures and devastated reefs around the world. Baum and Cobb expected destruction, but they were unprepared for the reality. They estimated that 80 percent of the corals were dead, 15 percent bleached but alive, and only 5 percent still healthy.[6] The dead coral was covered with fuzzy red algae. Baum has studied the reef for years because it was one of the healthiest in the world. The Kiritimati die-off is one of the worst casualties in this worldwide bleaching event.

increase of approximately 1.3 degrees Fahrenheit (0.72°C) in the past 100 years.[4] Temperatures have risen most rapidly since 1995. The Intergovernmental Panel on Climate Change (IPCC), in its 2013 report, predicts that surface temperatures of tropical oceans will rise 5.4 to 7.2 degrees Fahrenheit (3 to 4°C) by 2100 unless people decrease their input of greenhouse gases into the atmosphere. If ocean surface temperatures rise by just 1.8 degrees F (1°C), this could destroy all reefs by 2050.[5]

CORAL BLEACHING

Healthy corals have a strong relationship with their algal partners. But when high temperatures disrupt this relationship, zooxanthellae photosynthesis is affected. The algae begin to produce toxins. Tropical sunlight makes the problem worse by speeding up photosynthesis, which causes oxygen levels to increase. When oxygen levels become too high, this too begins poisoning the coral polyps. The corals respond by expelling the mostly brown zooxanthellae, leaving behind stark white, bleached coral skeletons. When large expanses of corals are bleached at once, the culprit is usually excessively high temperatures. But smaller segments of reefs often show bleaching. Localized bleaching can be caused by disease, chemicals, sediment coating, excess ultraviolet radiation from the sun, or decreased salinity from heavy rains or storms.

Thus, rising ocean temperatures are not the only cause of coral bleaching, but they are the main one. Most corals prefer temperatures between 73 and 84 degrees Fahrenheit (23 and 29°C), though some live in water up to 93 degrees Fahrenheit (34°C). Corals already live close to their upper limit of temperature tolerance. Even small increases above this limit, if they last long enough, can cause bleaching.

Bleached corals can recover if water temperatures come back down and zooxanthellae can repopulate the polyps' cells. But if temperatures stay high for weeks at a time and zooxanthellae do not return, the corals will die of starvation. During this time, the corals also become susceptible to many diseases. Macroalgae, or fast-growing, fleshy seaweeds, also begin taking over, forming a slimy coating over the reef. Macroalgae lack the three-dimensional structure of corals, providing much less shelter and habitat for reef animals.

CAN CORALS SURVIVE?

Corals are not helpless. Many coral colors—bright pinks, greens, and blues—are protective fluorescent compounds

WHICH REEFS MIGHT SURVIVE BLEACHING?
Scientists think reefs will be largely wiped out by climate change in the long term, but an Australian researcher has identified types of reefs most likely to survive short-term temperature increases. Nicholas Graham of Australia's James Cook University looked at the impact of the worldwide bleaching event of 1998. He found that 12 of 21 bleached reefs in the Seychelles were recovering. Using a model analyzing reef depth and physical complexity, Graham predicted with 98 percent accuracy that deeper reefs with greater complexity were most likely to survive.[7] Scientists suggest that, in the Great Barrier Reef, more northern, relatively pristine reefs farther offshore are most likely to recover. But Graham cautions that continued sediment dumping from port projects on the Queensland coast may still kill the reefs.

made by coral polyps. These and other compounds act as sunscreens, protecting corals and their zooxanthellae from excess ultraviolet radiation. Researchers think the algae make the compounds and transport them to the coral. The coral then modifies the compounds to make the sunscreen. But there are limits to the corals' ability to protect themselves. If sunlight is too intense, the coral pigments are unable to keep up, and the corals are damaged or they die. Also, sunscreens do not protect corals from high temperatures.

DOES BLEACHING REPLACE ZOOXANTHELLAE?

Until the 1990s, scientists thought all zooxanthellae belonged to the same species. But two scientists, Rob Rowan of the University of Guam and Nancy Knowlton of the Scripps Institution of Oceanography, used DNA studies to show that zooxanthellae are extremely diverse. Later studies showed that each coral species prefers a specific group of zooxanthellae, each with its own light and temperature tolerances. Two other scientists, Robert Buddemeier of the Kansas Geological Survey and Daphne Fautin of the University of Kansas, proposed an adaptive bleaching hypothesis, which suggests bleaching might be coral's way of replacing less heat-tolerant groups with more heat-tolerant ones. But many scientists are concerned that this kind of adaptive response will not be able to keep up with the rapidly rising temperatures.

Corals generally exist at temperatures only 1.8 to 3.6 degrees Fahrenheit (1 to 2°C) below their temperature limit. According to the 2013 IPCC report, the world is on track to reach this limit for most corals by mid-century. Different coral species have different temperature tolerances, suggesting some reefs might survive with different dominant species. However, because corals are already living so close to their tolerance limits, they may be unable to overcome rising temperature trends. Some scientists think corals may be able to repopulate their tissues with more heat-tolerant types of zooxanthellae after bleaching.

Most scientists are not optimistic about the chances for coral reef survival. In 1992, world leaders at the first United Nations convention on climate change recommended

Healthy - Dec 2014

Dying - Feb 2015

Dead - Aug 2015

Healthy, bleached and dying, and dead coral in American Samoa, 2014–2015

stabilizing atmospheric greenhouse gases to prevent global warming from exceeding a dangerous threshold. They said stabilization should happen over a time "sufficient to allow ecosystems to adapt naturally to climate change."[8] But conservationist and biodiversity expert Thomas Lovejoy of George Mason University says coral reefs are already past that threshold. Michael Oppenheimer of Princeton University sums up the fears of coral reef scientists: "From a global perspective, the level of warming is about to enter the danger zone for coral reefs and it is certainly arguable that it is already too late for some of these systems to 'adapt naturally.'"[9]

> **"We and others thought coral reefs would be the first global indicator of emergence of dangerous warming and events have borne out that expectation."[10]**
>
> *—Michael Oppenheimer,*
> *Princeton University*

Chapter
FIVE

A HOT ACID BATH

Climate change damages coral reefs by increasing ocean temperatures. But it has a second, equally damaging effect—it increases acidity. The greenhouse gas carbon dioxide first enters the atmosphere as a result of fossil fuel burning, which raises air temperatures. But not all carbon dioxide stays in the atmosphere. According to the Scripps Institution of Oceanography, between 2002 and 2011, 26 percent of the carbon released as carbon dioxide entered the oceans. (Another 28 percent went to plants, and 46 percent went into the atmosphere.) The total release

Carbon dioxide is invisible but has a large impact on the oceans.

of carbon into the atmosphere was 9.3 billion short tons (8.4 billion metric tons) per year. During that decade, approximately 2.5 billion short tons (2.3 billion metric tons) per year entered the oceans.[1]

THE pH SCALE

Not all substances are acids or bases. Acids are substances that produce hydrogen ions (H+) when they are dissolved in solution. Bases are substances that produce hydroxide ions (OH-) in solution. Water molecules break apart to produce one H+ ion and one OH- ion; that is, water has equal concentrations of the two ions. So pure water is a neutral substance, neither acidic nor basic. The pH scale ranges from 0 to 14. The middle value, 7, is neutral—the pH of pure water. Values above 7 are increasingly basic, with 14 being the most basic. Values below 7 are increasingly acidic, with 0 being the most acidic. Each whole value is 10 times the previous value. That is, pH 8 is 10 times more basic than pH 7, and pH 6 is 10 times more acidic than pH 7.

CHANGING OCEAN pH LEVELS

Dissolved carbon dioxide reacts with ocean water to form carbonic acid (H_2CO_3). Acidity is measured using the pH scale, which goes from 0 to 14, with 0 being the most acidic and 14 being the most basic, or alkaline. The middle of the scale, 7, is neutral—the pH of pure water. Ocean water is slightly basic. Since the beginning of the Industrial Revolution in the mid-1700s, accumulating carbon dioxide has dropped the average ocean pH from 8.2 to 8.1. It is likely to drop another 0.3 to 0.4 pH units by 2100.[2] This seems like a very small decrease, and it doesn't even make the oceans acidic, just less basic. So, one might think, what's the big deal?

To understand why such a seemingly small decrease is a big deal, it is necessary to understand how the pH scale works. The scale is logarithmic, not linear. This means each decrease of one unit represents a tenfold decrease in the actual value. In other words, a pH of 7 is 10 times more acidic than a pH

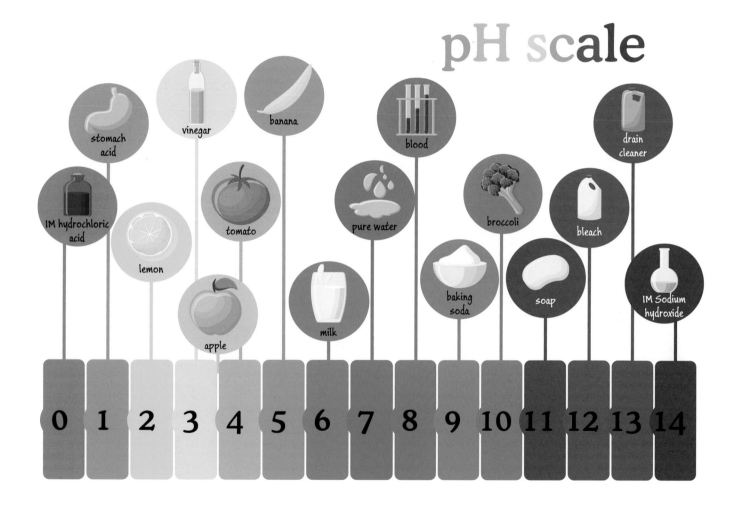

pH scale

stomach acid

vinegar

banana

blood

drain cleaner

1M hydrochloric acid

lemon

tomato

pure water

broccoli

bleach

apple

milk

baking soda

soap

1M Sodium hydroxide

0 1 2 3 4 5 6 7 8 9 10 11 12 13 14

Universal indicator solution is a common chemical detector used to reveal a mixture's acidity that changes the color of the solution as shown.

of 8. A pH of 6 is 100 (10 × 10) times more acidic than a pH of 8. If human activities continue to add carbon dioxide at current rates and seawater reaches a pH of 7.7 or 7.8 by the end of the century, it will be 120 percent more acidic than it is now. This is more acidic than at any time during the past 20 million years.[3]

CORALS AND RISING ACIDITY

Changes in pH and calcium carbonate affect organism reproduction and growth, especially in corals, which have calcium carbonate skeletons. The reaction of acids with calcium carbonate interferes with the ability of corals to build skeletons. The 0.1 decrease in ocean pH since preindustrial times has already decreased coral calcification rates by 20 percent.

Every day, the oceans absorb about 22 million short tons (20 million metric tons) of carbon dioxide, or approximately one-third of the amount humans produce.[4]

Crustose coralline algae form brilliant patches of pink and red on rocks and coral. The worms are feather-duster worms.

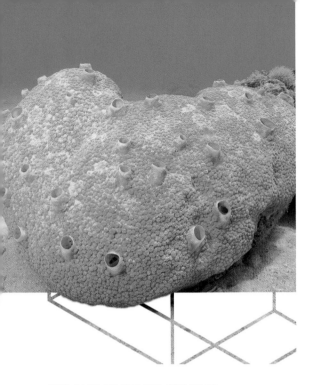

THE RISE OF BORING SPONGES

Boring sponges break down materials made of calcium carbonate. Their larvae settle on coral skeletons and the shells of mollusks and other reef creatures. They secrete sulfuric acid, which eats away at the calcium carbonate, chipping off pieces and etching tunnels and pock-marks that weaken the skeleton. In this way, they recycle dead and diseased skeletons, making room for new settlement. Unlike corals, boring sponges seem unaffected by rising temperature and acidity. This might become a problem. A healthy reef can balance growth and erosion. But on a warming, acidified reef, the balance might be tipped in favor of erosion by boring sponges. This is already happening in Caribbean reefs.

If ocean pH decreases by another 0.3 to 0.4 pH units by the end of this century, rates are expected to decrease to 40 to 60 percent of normal.[5]

Hard corals, the major reef builders, also show changes in metabolism and cellular activity when acidity increases. Building skeletons takes longer and uses more energy. Increasing acidity also causes the loss of zooxanthellae. Zooxanthellae that stay show a 60 percent drop in photosynthesis.[6] This makes less energy available to coral polyps when they need more. They produce weaker skeletons that dissolve, crumble, or break apart more easily. Crustose coralline algae, which help cement the reef, are even more sensitive to pH changes than corals. They show greatly reduced productivity and calcification and may be damaged before the corals are.

Reefs need a healthy balance between reef building and erosion. If building occurs faster, a reef grows; if erosion occurs faster, it degrades. Some scientists think that, by mid-century, reef erosion will be occurring faster than reef building. Coral reef communities may be replaced with communities dominated by non-corals such as seaweed.

OTHER ORGANISMS

Organisms throughout a reef produce shells or skeletons using some form of calcium carbonate, and all are affected by increasing acidity. Sea stars and sea urchins build internal skeletons from a form of calcium carbonate that dissolves more rapidly than the form used by corals. In acidic water, they build weaker shells and are therefore more likely to be crushed or eaten. Tiny, shelled zooplankton called foraminifera are critical to food webs and to the carbon cycle on reefs. Because they reproduce rapidly, some scientists thought they might adapt to acidity more readily than larger animals. But lab experiments show their shells dissolve too rapidly. Coccolithophores, a group of phytoplankton, appear able to adapt to rising acid. In a yearlong study covering 700 generations, they eventually adapted and grew strong shells in warmer, more acidic conditions.[7]

"Are we fighting a losing battle? Quite possibly climate change might have passed the point of no return. What is clear is that any solution to climate change is also the solution to coral reef recovery."[8]

–Marcia Creary, Centre for Marine Sciences, University of the West Indies, Jamaica

Excess acid stresses non-shelled organisms, too. Fish take dissolved carbonic acid into their bodies, lowering the pH of their cells and body fluids. They remove the excess acid through their gills, kidneys, and intestines. This requires energy, which they then cannot use for growing, reproducing, escaping predators, or catching food.

Jellyfish compete for food with fish and other predators. In the last few decades, many newspaper stories have documented population explosions of jellyfish. The population

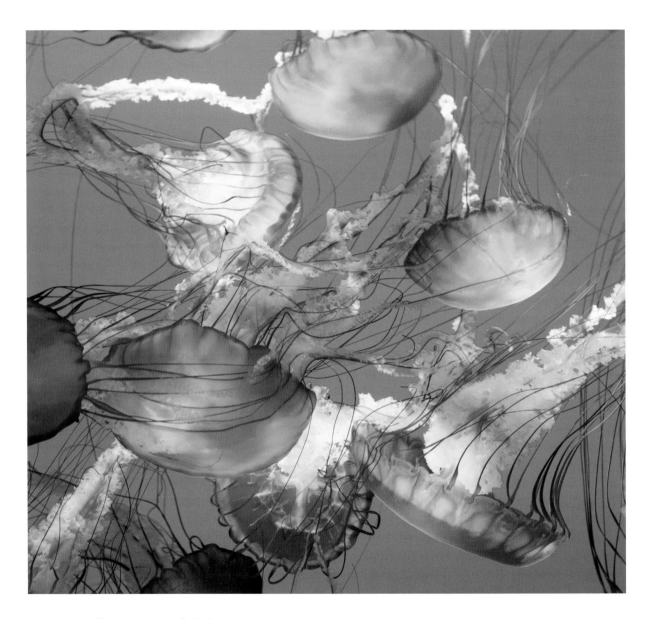

Some jellyfish have painful, dangerous stings.

booms appear related to ocean pollution, declining fish populations, and increases in temperature and acidity. With no shells or skeletons to dissolve and no negative response to high temperature or acidity, jellyfish seem poised to overtake many future marine ecosystems, including coral reefs.

Ecologist Roger Bradbury has a very depressing view of the future of coral reefs. He cites the combined stresses of overfishing, acidification, and pollution as the major factors that will destroy reefs. What will remain, he says, will be a slimy, "algal-dominated hard ocean bottom . . . with lots of microbial life . . . few fish but lots of jellyfish grazing on the microbes."[9] His vision is not an appealing prospect, especially when compared with the wondrous, colorful reefs of today.

ILI ILI BUA BUA

On Normanby Island in Papua New Guinea is a village called Ili Ili Bua Bua, which translates to Water Water Bubble Bubble. The village is named for the carbon dioxide that continuously bubbles out of volcanic cracks in the shallow seafloor. Coral reefs around these cracks provide a preview of how reefs might look in 100 years, as carbon dioxide continues to increase ocean acidity. Reefs near the bubbling cracks contain only massive brown boulder corals. There are no beautiful, brightly colored, branching corals and no colorful, darting fish. Nearest the cracks, there are no corals at all. There is only sand, rubble and algae.

HOW ACID DISSOLVES CORALS

All life depends on chemical reactions, which are extremely sensitive to small changes in pH and other chemical factors. The chemical processes that cause ocean acidification and dissolve corals begin when carbon dioxide dissolves into seawater. It forms carbonic acid, which then ionizes (breaks apart) to form a hydrogen ion and a bicarbonate ion:

$$CO_2 + H_2O \longrightarrow H_2CO_3 \longrightarrow H^+ + HCO_3^-$$

carbon dioxide + water $\longrightarrow$ carbonic acid $\longrightarrow$ hydrogen ion + bicarbonate ion

The addition of hydrogen ions (H+) increases the acidity (lowers the pH) of ocean water. The hydrogen ions react with carbonate present in the water to produce more bicarbonate, using up carbonate in the seawater.

Hydrogen ions are more strongly attracted to carbonate than to calcium in seawater. So bicarbonate ions form in preference to calcium carbonate ($CaCO_3$), a solid. Corals need carbonate to make coral skeletons, but they cannot extract it from bicarbonate. So this chemical reaction decreases the carbonate available to corals. If the water is too acidic—that is, if there is an excess of hydrogen ions—the hydrogen ions will begin breaking down existing calcium carbonate molecules. That is, they will dissolve already existing coral skeletons.

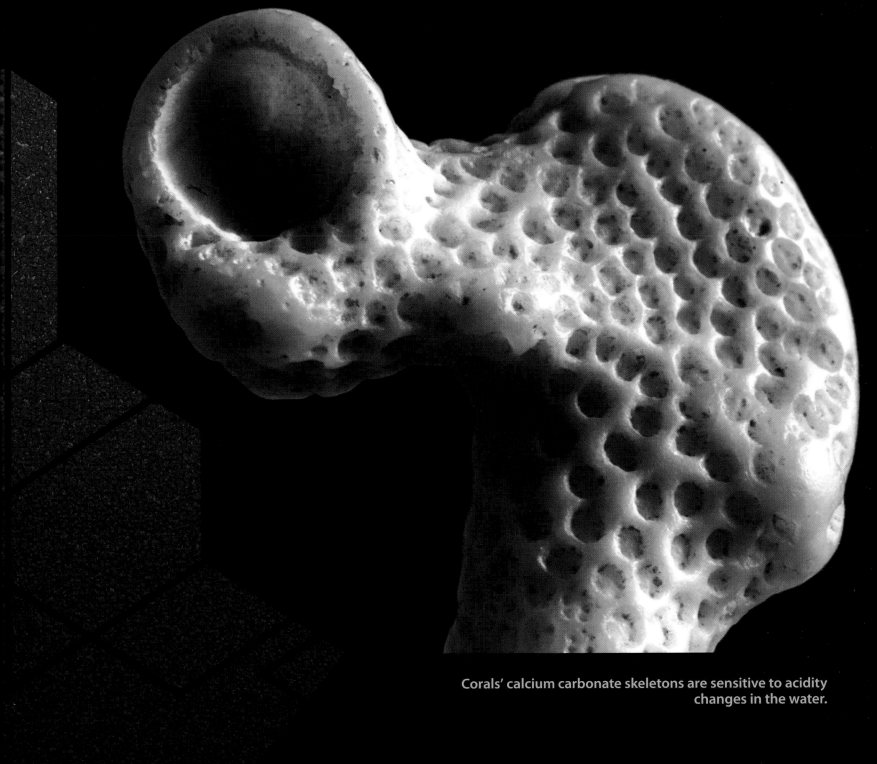

Corals' calcium carbonate skeletons are sensitive to acidity
changes in the water.

SIX

THREATS FROM OCEAN POLLUTION AND DISEASE

Since the mid-1900s, climate change has gone from a minor worry among scientific experts to a full-blown, worldwide crisis. The rate of climate change is increasing. In the past several decades, changes have occurred much

An underwater pipe spews pollution near a coral reef.

more quickly than expected. Rates are expected to increase even more rapidly in coming decades. Rising reef temperatures and increasing acidity are seriously stressing coral reefs. This is a long-term change affecting reefs all over the world.

Climate change would be bad enough if it were the reefs' only problem. But reefs are also threatened by local stresses caused by human activity. These stresses are interlinked and are happening along with climate change. In combination, their total harm to reefs is even greater than if all the individual effects were added together.

POLLUTION ON THE REEF

"Coral reefs have for a long time been considered to be the litmus, the canary in the coal mine, which foretells substantial and deleterious [harmful] changes happening to the Earth system."[2]
—Charles Sheppard, Coral Reefs: A Very Short Introduction

According to the National Oceanic and Atmospheric Administration (NOAA), approximately 80 percent of coral reef pollution in the Caribbean comes from onshore activities.[1] The same types of pollution are found worldwide. A major problem is nutrient enrichment, which is the addition of too many nutrients to an ecosystem. Humans add sewage from coastal communities and fertilizer or waste from agriculture or aquaculture operations. Nutrient enrichment speeds the growth of large, fleshy seaweeds. The seaweeds grow much more rapidly than corals, take up reef space, and shade the corals. Since most grazing animals will not eat seaweeds, the seaweeds quickly outcompete corals and take over the reef.

Algae overgrows corals in the Florida Keys.

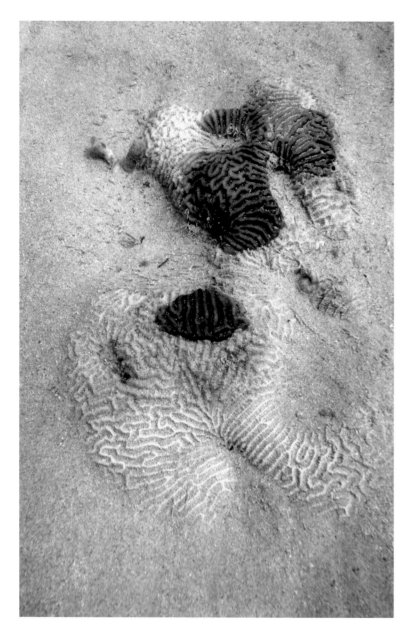

Coral bleaching and dying as it is buried under sand, Coral Bay, Australia

Excess nutrients also cause phytoplankton blooms on the reef. This decreases light underwater, making it more difficult for the corals' zooxanthellae to photosynthesize. Later, the blooms lead to less oxygen in the water, as bacteria use oxygen to break down the phytoplankton.

Pesticides and toxic chemicals often run into nearshore waters and over coral reefs. Pesticides poison zooplankton and other reef inhabitants. Herbicides damage or destroy zooxanthellae, free-living phytoplankton, and nearby algal and seagrass communities. Industries release toxic chemicals into the water. These chemicals damage nearly every life process in corals, including growth, reproduction, feeding, cell structure, and defensive responses.

Finally, sediment is a major concern on reefs around the world. Some sediment is soil runoff that smothers reefs. It comes from land-based construction projects, deforestation, and erosion. Some sediment is loose silt stirred up from the ocean floor. Dredging in the shallow ocean around reefs can devastate reefs. When sediment is suspended in the water, it increases cloudiness, reduces oxygen, and releases toxins and bacteria. It also drastically reduces the amount of light reaching the reef, which decreases photosynthesis. As sediments settle, they can bury corals alive. Corals try to remove sediment by producing mucus, which takes a lot of energy and weakens them.

CORAL DISEASES

Bacteria, viruses, and fungi are always present on the reef. When corals are stressed by other factors, these microbes take advantage. Coral disease has spiked since approximately 2000, apparently due to the high stress from increasing reef temperatures and human-caused pollution. A significant increase in coral disease followed the 2002 mass bleaching event on the GBR. Another cause is excess nutrients (primarily nitrogen and phosphorus), which can come from surface runoff. Excess nutrients both increase corals' likelihood of catching diseases and speed up the disease process. A third cause, physical damage, often happens during storms and

SEDIMENT ON SAINT LUCIA

The small eastern Caribbean island of Saint Lucia is vulnerable to sediment pollution because of its steep mountains, which erode rapidly. In 1995, a marine protected area (MPA) was created to protect the island's coral reefs by preventing removal of any organisms, including fish and corals. By 2001, fish populations had quadrupled inside the reserves. However, coral cover had declined by 36 to 45 percent.[3] The coral succumbed to disease, bleaching, and hurricane damage three years in a row, compounded by constant sedimentation. When the study areas were sampled again in 2011, there had been another sharp decline in coral cover, and seaweed was increasing. These changes were directly associated with sediment.

WHITE BAND DISEASE

White band disease has caused staggering losses in the Caribbean. In the 1980s and 1990s, white band disease destroyed nearly all of the region's most impressive corals, the *Acropora*, or staghorn and elkhorn corals. There have been no mass mortalities on this scale for at least 3,000 to 4,000 years.[4] Both staghorn and elkhorn corals are now listed as threatened under the US Endangered Species Act. So far, scientists have found no cause for white band disease, which appears to exist in two forms, caused by different microbes. But a 2015 study by the Florida Institute of Technology implicates rising ocean temperatures due to climate change in the spread of the disease. The disease is more common where the waters have been warming the most and where they do not cool off during the winter.

cyclones, which break corals and increase the murkiness of the water.

Coral diseases are visible as color changes on the corals. Black band disease, red band disease, and yellow blotch or yellow band disease produce bands or blotches of these colors on the coral surface. These expand over the coral, consuming living tissue and leaving behind a white, bleached skeleton. Other diseases include rapid wasting, white band, white plague, and white pox, which cause large patches of living coral to fall off, showing the skeleton beneath. The exposed skeleton is rapidly overgrown by algae, and the coral rarely recovers.

Determining the causes of coral diseases is difficult. For example, black band disease is known to infect at least 40 coral species around the world. It is highly contagious. It spreads more rapidly in warmer waters and where there are excess nutrients. Researchers found that black band disease is caused not by a single bacterium, but by a mix of more than 50 marine bacteria plus a number of marine fungi. This mass of pathogens appears to work together, forming a millimeter-thick mat that covers the coral, both poisoning and suffocating it. Many coral diseases seem to function in this way, with a mass of pathogens killing corals by crawling over the coral surface, creating toxic, oxygen-free zones.

PLASTICS ON THE REEF

Most environmental pollutants eventually break down. Bacteria and fungi decompose sewage and toxic chemicals into harmless or less toxic forms. But microbes do not degrade plastics; only ultraviolet light does. As plastics in the oceans are exposed to sunlight, they eventually break down into many tiny pieces. Unfortunately, many of these pieces contain toxic chemicals, such as bisphenol A (BPA). Animals often eat these pieces, or they wash up on shorelines.

Plastics have been accumulating in the oceans since the end of World War II (1939–1945). They tend to collect in huge circular currents, or gyres, in the major oceans. One of these is the Great Pacific Garbage Patch, where Captain Charles Moore of the Algalita foundation has measured six pounds (2.7 kg) of plastic for every pound of phytoplankton. The garbage patch covers an area twice the size of Texas and is still growing. The United Nations Environment Programme says there are now 46,000 pieces of plastic for every one square mile (2.6 sq km) of ocean, and this plastic circulates down to a depth of 100 feet (30 m).[5] Plastic pollution reaches every part of the oceans, including coral reefs.

"In the future, the twentieth century will be clearly visible in the geologic record by an indelible layer of plastic, as if a vast rain of synthetic meteorites had crashed to the earth."[6]

—The Crochet Coral Reef, a project of the Institute for Figuring

Plastic trash litters beaches around the world.

According to the environmental advocacy organization Greenpeace, every year one million seabirds and 100,000 marine mammals die from eating plastic. Filter feeders, including corals, draw ocean water into their bodies and filter out edible plankton. Now they also draw in tiny plastic fragments, which contain toxins such as pesticides and industrial chemicals. Tiny plastic pellets, or microplastics, can have toxin concentrations up to one million times the levels found in seawater—and these pellets are entering ocean food chains.[7] Researcher Nora Hall found that corals eat microplastics at rates only slightly lower than they eat plankton. Plastic enters the polyps' digestive tissue, where it likely interferes with corals' ability to digest normal food. The corals will starve to death, as birds and other larger animals are already doing.

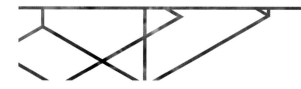

HOW MUCH PLASTIC IS THERE?

In 1975, the National Academy of Sciences estimated that perhaps 0.1 percent of all plastics ended up in the oceans. Now, they know things are much worse. New calculations suggest that the percentage varies between perhaps 15 and 40 percent— or 4.4 and 13.2 million short tons (4 and 12 million metric tons) per year. Scientists still have no idea what happens to 99 percent of ocean plastic or how it affects ocean life or the human food supply. Plus, the amount of plastic entering the oceans is expected to double between 2015 and 2025.[8]

Coral reefs are the most biodiverse and productive ecosystems in the oceans. Through fishing, tourism, and other ecosystem services, they support more people per unit area than any other ecosystem. Their destruction, or even loss of biodiversity, profoundly affects the human communities surrounding them. The pollution that stresses and kills them is caused by people, and it could be stopped by them. The question is, will pollution be stopped in time, or will efforts be too little, too late?

Coral reef tourism is popular but can damage the ecosystem.

Chapter

SEVEN

OVERFISHING AND TOURISM

Worldwide, 58 percent of coral reefs are within 30 minutes of a human settlement.[1] A 2016 study looked at the density of human populations around coral reefs and the density of those reefs' fish populations. Not surprisingly, they found that more people meant fewer fish. In general, accessible reefs—those easily reached by people—show the most signs of degradation, while less accessible reefs remain more pristine. Reefs are routinely degraded by overfishing, destructive fishing practices, careless and unsustainable tourism, and the global aquarium

WHO ARE THE REEF PREDATORS?

Barracuda are strong, fast-moving, and curious. They are long and muscular, with large heads and snouts and spiky teeth. They are large enough to grab other reef predators, such as snappers. Groupers, *above*, are huge predators who feed on spiny lobster, crabs, and smaller fish. They have large mouths that create suction when opened. They are friendly to people, following divers and feeding from their hands. They are easy prey for spear fishers and are now almost extinct throughout the Caribbean. Grunts, hawkfish, snappers, and jacks are smaller predators that feed on crustaceans, small fish, and sometimes sea urchins. Jacks swim in schools to protect themselves against barracudas. They have deep, somewhat compressed bodies with spiky, curved tailfins and a silvery color. Snappers are aggressive, voracious predators. The beautifully colored red snapper is a popular game fish in the Gulf of Mexico and the Caribbean. Within the reef, shy moray eels hide in crevices and dart out to catch octopi and other reef dwellers. Sharks, once common on Caribbean reefs, are now almost entirely absent.

trade. Coral is also mined and used in canals, fish ponds, and house and street foundations. It is even sold as a souvenir.

OVERFISHED AND BLASTED REEFS

Almost all of the world's coral reefs are overfished. Caribbean coral reef fisheries employ approximately 300,000 people and add $395 million per year in US dollars to the Caribbean economy.[2] Many fishers turn to reef fishing after losing jobs in other sectors. The Caribbean reef fishery industry has been declining since the 1980s. The most valuable species in the Caribbean are the spiny lobster and queen conch, and both are now overcaught. Some of the most desirable reef fish are now listed on the IUCN Red List, an international list that classifies species according to their risk of extinction. In addition to reduced fish stocks, the reef itself is undergoing profound changes. Fish are smaller, and more are from lower in the food chain. Many reefs are now dominated by seaweed. Biodiversity is lower, so reefs are less able to recover from stress. The physical structure of the corals is degrading.

East Africa also shows how overfishing damages reefs. In the countries of Kenya, Mozambique, and Tanzania, hundreds of thousands of coastal residents make their living by fishing, and about the same number are employed in marketing and processing the catch. Fish, shrimp, crabs, and mollusks are the residents' major sources of protein. Over the entire region, 500 species of fish are harvested, providing approximately 200,000 short tons (180,000 metric tons) of fish per year.[3]

Most East African fishers (90 to 95 percent in Mozambique) use simple gear such as hook and line, spears, nets, or woven fish traps. The most serious problem is the increasing use of destructive fishing methods, including dynamite and small-meshed nets, which destroy both coral reefs and seagrass beds. These practices along the coasts of Kenya and Tanzania have decreased coral reef fish catches by 30 to 40 percent.[4]

In dynamite or blast fishing, fish are killed by the shock wave and scooped off the surface. Blast fishing uses bombs made from local materials. Even a relatively small beer-bottle bomb leaves a crater approximately 3 to 6.5 feet (1 to 2 m) across and kills 50 to 80 percent of corals surrounding the blast area.[5] A blasted reef may take several hundred years to recover. Although illegal, blast fishing is practiced in

BLAST FISHING IN TANZANIA

As of 2015, Tanzania was the only African country where large-scale blast fishing still widely occurred. The practice has been illegal since 1970, but mining and construction activity make it easy to obtain dynamite. A fisher can make $1,800 in profit with a single blast. Researchers recorded 300 blasts within 30 days in the spring of 2015, 60 percent of them within 50 miles (80 km) of Tanzania's largest city, Dar es Salaam. This measurement is conservative, researchers say. Most blasts occur in very shallow water, where their hydrophones cannot record. According to Greg Wagner of the University of Dar es Salaam, "The overall impact of dynamite fishing on coral reefs in Tanzania has been devastating."[6] The blasts turn reefs into rubble, ruining tourism and destroying the livelihoods of fishers. The government wants to control this illegal activity and the trade that goes with it. However, it is dealing with few resources, confusion over who can enforce the law, and lenient sentences for those convicted.

30 countries in Southeast Asia, Oceania, and East Africa. Most countries want to eliminate blast fishing because of its damage to tourism and the legal fishing industry. Kenya has been very successful at eliminating dynamite fishing by making it harder for people to buy explosives. Cambodia has also been successful, but in other Southeast Asian countries, particularly Indonesia and the Philippines, the practice is still common. Fishers say these methods are necessary to compete with trawlers and to catch enough fish on the already overfished reefs.

ROBBING REEFS TO STOCK AQUARIUMS

Worldwide, more than two million people keep aquariums.[7] Every year, more than 11 million fish and millions of other reef dwellers are taken from coral reefs to supply the 700,000 US aquarium hobbyists alone. More than one million reef animals come from Hawaiian coral reefs. The entire reef is damaged by overharvesting and the use of cyanide to stun fish for capture. Nine fish die for every one that reaches a hobby tank. Most of those who reach a tank die within weeks or months, from stress due to disease, cramped conditions, improper food, or inexperienced keepers. When these animals are removed, reefs become imbalanced, and individual species crash. Yellow tang populations in Hawaii have declined by 70 to 90 percent.[8]

Hawaii serves as an example of the destruction by the aquarium trade of reefs around the world. The out-of-control collection of reef organisms is causing once-common reef species to disappear, upsetting reef balance and destroying the ability of reefs to serve as

Indonesian officials burn several foreign fishing vessels caught blast fishing.

nurseries for young organisms. The aquarium trade is virtually unregulated. In Hawaii, for example, removing corals is illegal, but for a $50 annual permit, commercial collectors can remove any other living animal on the reefs. Ninety-nine percent of Hawaii's reefs are now endangered.[9] Many reefs are being suffocated by algae, since the herbivores that keep algae in check are being removed.

CARELESS TOURISTS DESTROY REEFS

Coral reef tourism brings in considerable income. However, tourism can destroy the very reefs on which it depends. Heedless swimmers and divers break off pieces of coral, as do boaters who use their heavy anchors carelessly. Hotels and resorts release untreated sewage or other wastewater into the ocean, increasing algal growth. On some reefs, including those in Fiji, interactive diving, or

Yellow tang are a popular aquarium fish, but they are a key species in the reef ecosystem, keeping algal growth down and providing food for larger animals.

Divers in Malaysia feed a school of fish.

dive tours on which tourists can feed the fish, are changing fish behavior. Fish now expect handouts from divers. This is affecting the health of the reef and disrupting food webs. Some fish are becoming more aggressive, fighting each other and breaking corals.

The Mamanuca Environment Society (MES) of Fiji is dealing with the dangers of tourism by educating tourists and providing them with guidelines for respecting the reef. The MES has shown it can reduce reef damage by 95 percent by informing tourists of proper reef protocol.[10]

Coral reefs are being crushed or stripped of their corals, fish, and other organisms, resulting in damage to their beauty and the ecosystem. It takes decades, even centuries, to rebuild a reef. But this destruction is combined with chemical pollution and the stresses of high temperatures and increasing acidity due to climate change. This overwhelming convergence of dangers threatens the very existence of coral reefs.

HOW TO POISON A REEF

Surprisingly, poison is used to capture fish alive. Poisons, most commonly cyanide and bleach, are squirted into reef crevices. They stun or kill the fish, which float to the surface. Those that survive are captured for the aquarium or food trade. Some individual fish survive because they get a small dose. But many fish are taken, and the whole reef receives a huge poison load. The corals are bleached and many die, as do other reef animals. In the Philippines, an estimated 2.2 million pounds (1 million kg) of cyanide have been poured onto reefs in the last 50 years, and these reefs are now devastated.[11]

EIGHT

REEF CONSERVATION AND MANAGEMENT

G iven the dangers facing coral reefs, what can be done to save them? The major dangers of rising temperature and acidity resulting from climate change can only be solved by worldwide action to decrease carbon pollution. But sensible

Protected areas must be respected in order to keep corals safe.

HOW TO REHABILITATE A REEF

Mars Inc., the candy company, is carrying out reef rehabilitation in the Pacific Ocean's Coral Triangle. The Mars Ambassador Program conducts community outreach programs around the world, including science and conservation efforts, in areas where the candy company operates and sources ingredients. Mars is rebuilding reefs devastated by blast fishing and cyanide fishing. First, workers build a new reef foundation using "spiders," square-meter pieces of rebar coated with adhesive and covered with a mixture of sand and calcium carbonate. Live coral fragments left after bombing are replanted on the spiders, which divers then return to the ocean floor. They arrange the spiders in an intricate web and tie them together, replacing the bombed reef. Brian Records, a Mars employee, participated in reef rehab on the island of Badi, off the coast of Makassar, Indonesia. When he returned a year later, Records said, "Spiders from prior years are almost unrecognizable and completely covered in coral, proving success."[1]

coral reef management and conservation can keep reefs healthier so they will be better able to withstand the stresses of climate change. Coral reef conservation includes two basic steps: protection and rehabilitation. First, reefs should be protected by eliminating, or at least decreasing, the stresses causing the damage. Second, because reefs around the world have already suffered extensive damage, rehabilitation is needed to repair them. Strategies include managing watersheds and wetlands, decreasing pollution, regulating industries that remove corals from reefs, and preventing other activities such as destructive fishing. These strategies involve three types of control: regulation, management, and creating protected areas. Regulation and management are related: regulation refers to a set of rules that govern the trade in reef fisheries or wildlife, and management is the implementation and enforcement of conservation measures, including regulations.

KEY CONSERVATION STRATEGIES

Coral reefs are particularly difficult to manage and regulate. Common practices such as dynamite and cyanide fishing are unsustainable and extremely damaging to coral reefs. Often

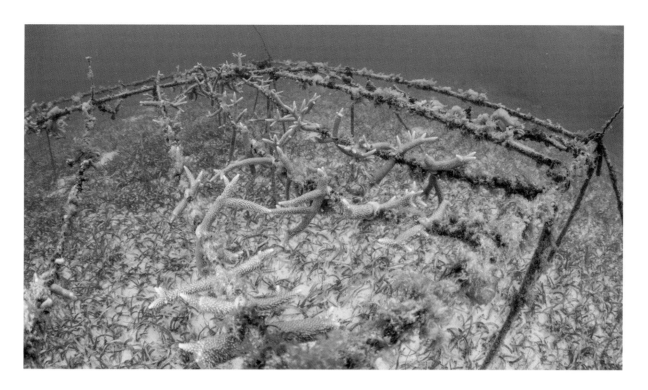

Corals grow on an artificial framework, helping revitalize a Caribbean reef.

many countries are included within a single region of reefs, such as the Caribbean reef system. This makes regulation more complex and requires international agreements. Even reef biodiversity increases the problems. Hundreds of species are harvested instead of a single species as in, say, the tuna fishing industry. This makes laws such as catch limits unfeasible, since a limit would be needed for each species.

Regulation methods are based on local needs and conditions. One country or region might restrict the type of fishing gear. Others might set bans that prevent the harvest of certain species. Still others might limit total harvests of a species by setting quotas, called

A NOAA Coral Reef Management Fellow records coral bleaching in Guam.

a total allowable catch. Some regulations are aimed at protecting biodiversity, allowing a region to recover, or protecting individual species. These include prohibiting fishing in certain zones or setting size limits for a species.

Marine species are managed on several levels. The United Nations Convention on the Law of the Sea regulates open-ocean activities. However, it also establishes exclusive economic zones. These zones give individual countries control over nearshore waters, including coral reefs. That is, each country makes its own rules. But these regulations are implemented and enforced locally, by individual managers and fishers, so their success varies.

In the United States, the major government agency working to protect coral reefs is NOAA. NOAA's Coral Reef Conservation Program protects coral reefs both nationally and internationally. The program concentrates on reef problems: unsustainable fishing, climate change, and land-based pollution. The online database CoRIS (Coral Reef Information System) makes NOAA's coral reef data available around the world. The program maps and monitors reefs. It uses models to forecast disasters such as coral bleaching. It also develops management plans and provides training and workshops.

Nonprofit organizations also work on coral reef protection. The National Fish and Wildlife Foundation (NFWF) was created by Congress, but it collaborates with federal and private agencies. It supplies grant funds for conservation efforts. It works on reducing land-based pollution. It also develops management plans that have measurable goals, improving management of protected areas. The NFWF supports programs totaling $34 million in 39 countries.[2]

Scientists at Defenders of Wildlife do research on coral reef ecology and develop new management approaches. They try to implement sustainable collection methods that

"We need to better understand the human dimensions of reefs if we are to effectively manage them—this includes understanding peoples' values, aspirations, and needs and how these influence the ways they use and manage reefs."[3]

—Joshua Cinner, research fellow, James Cook University, Australia

do not damage reefs. They also promote the use of the US Endangered Species Act (ESA) to define and list endangered reef species. They advocate for the ESA, work to make sure it is enforced, and look for ways to make it more effective. The Center for Biological Diversity has also been active in protecting coral reefs. In 2006, it campaigned successfully to have elkhorn and staghorn corals listed under the ESA—the first species listed because of vulnerability to global warming. The group later filed a lawsuit to ensure the corals 3,000 square miles (7,770 sq km) of protected habitat. It has also filed petitions to protect some reef fish, including the orange clownfish and some damselfish, under the ESA.

MANAGING THE AQUARIUM TRADE

The challenges of regulating the aquarium trade illustrate the difficulties of reef conservation. The aquarium trade has several differences from the food fishery trade, which has established management methods. The value of aquarium fish is based on the individual fish rather than on biomass (total weight of fish), and the animals must remain alive. Also, aquarium collectors prefer juveniles and brightly colored males. Targeting these groups affects the age structure and sex ratios of the fish on the reef, making it more difficult to restore populations.

Many different species are removed from reefs. They include more than 1,800 fish species, hundreds of corals, and more than 500 invertebrates.[4] Many species are rare, and it is difficult to monitor population sizes or changes. Most locations have few or no regulations. Where regulations exist, reporting is inaccurate, making the laws difficult to

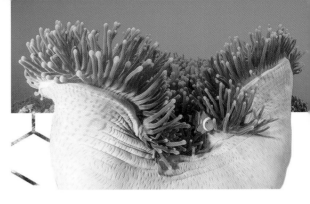

enforce. In addition, many collectors move from reef to reef and may never return, so they have little incentive to practice conservation measures.

MARINE PROTECTED AREAS

In recent years, governments have become concerned about the fate of the world's coral reefs and other tropical ecosystems. The number and size of Marine Protected Areas (MPAs) is rising as people realize the danger these ecosystems face. An MPA is similar to a national park for the oceans. MPAs single out regions of the oceans that are home to the most unique and critical marine habitats. They try to ensure these regions are safe from overexploitation, pollution, and other human-caused dangers. They provide refuges, spawning habitats, and nurseries for marine organisms. They protect biodiversity and allow stressed ecosystems to recover. This helps reefs build resilience and become more able to withstand climate change. In the process, people catch more fish and the culture and livelihoods of surrounding human communities benefit.

REDUCING LAND-BASED POLLUTION

Many threats facing reefs involve land-based pollutants. Preventing this pollution requires cooperation with governments, industries, and individuals. Australian conservationists Clive Wilkinson and Jon Brodie (with the cooperation of the United Nations, NOAA, and Australian agencies) developed a management handbook to help coastal resource managers understand how coastal management affects nearby coral reefs. Their recommendations centered on sediment, the top pollutant, followed by excess nutrients, which often come with sediment. Excess nutrients can lead to water-discoloring algae blooms, which can disrupt ecosystems. They cautioned that keeping these pollutants away from the reef requires identifying sources, monitoring flows, and interacting with farmers and foresters to lessen the runoff from eroding hillsides, agricultural lands, and other sources. It also requires scientific evidence relating to the ecosystems, pollutants, sources, and their interactions. These are difficult problems that cannot be solved quickly or easily, but they must be tackled if coral reefs are to survive.

Marine Park Police of Thailand patrol the Marine Protected Area in Krabi in the Andaman Sea, looking for illegal fishing or other unauthorized use of the park.

Worldwide, as of 2010, the approximately 5,000 MPAs covered an area of 1.1 million square miles (2.85 million sq km). This represents about 0.8 percent of the world's oceans, and 2 percent of the ocean that is governed by any country. Of these MPAs, just under 10 percent consist of marine reserves, or areas that cannot be harvested.[5]

In the United States, various types of MPAs have different purposes and are established at all levels of government. Marine sanctuaries, estuarine research reserves, ocean parks, and marine wildlife refuges are a few types. One MPA might protect a region from all human activity, while another is managed as a sustainable fishery. But, according to the National Ocean Service, the goal of all MPAs is to "conserve, manage, and protect" selected marine regions.[6]

Committed marine scientists and interested people around the world are working hard to protect the few remaining pristine reefs, and to manage the many reefs that are under siege from human activities. But the task is great. In addition, none of these efforts directly deal with the threat that looms over all reefs—the rising temperatures and acidity resulting from climate change.

THE NEWEST MPAS

In 2015 and 2016, several countries established new Marine Protected Areas to preserve and protect pristine ocean areas, especially coral reefs. These are shown in the table.

COUNTRY	LOCATION	SIZE
Palau	Western Pacific Ocean	193,000 square miles (500,000 sq km)[7]
Chile	Desventuradas Islands, west of Chile	115,000 square miles (298,000 sq km)[8]
United Kingdom	Pitcairn Islands, South Pacific	322,000 square miles (834,000 sq km)[9]
United States	Northwestern Hawaii	583,000 square miles (1,510,000 sq km)[10]

Chapter NINE

ARE CORAL REEFS DOOMED?

I t's obvious that many coral reefs are not in good shape. They are trying to survive under what seems to be a never-ending onslaught of threats and disasters. But how serious is the problem? Can at least some coral reefs be saved, and if so, how?

Coral bleaching threatens reefs in Thailand's Phi Phi Islands, a popular tourist destination.

WHAT THE DOOMSDAY EXPERTS SAY

As early as 2009, several experts said coral reefs were doomed. They all described the same factors that in the next few decades will likely turn reefs from colorful, biodiverse, thriving communities into "giant piles of slime-covered rubbish," as reporter David Adam put it.[1] These factors begin with the local stresses that reefs face every day, from sediments to sewage to overfishing. They end with the specter of climate change, as reefs become warmer and bleaching events more frequent. The final nail in the coffin is rising acidity and crumbling reefs as calcium carbonate becomes less available and corals are less able to build strong skeletons. On the Great Barrier Reef, calcification rates dropped 14 percent between 1990 and 2009—and acidity is still rising on the reefs.[2]

As these coral researchers view the situation, their conclusions are grim. David Obura, an expert from Kenya, says, "I don't think reefs have much of a chance. And what's happening to reefs is a parable of what is going to happen to everything else."[3] Australian marine biologist Charlie Veron sees no hope. Coral reefs will go first, he says, and other ecosystems will follow, leading to a mass extinction of tropical marine life. Alex Rogers, of Oxford University, sees "an absolute guarantee of their annihilation."[4]

Ecologist Roger Bradbury of Australian National University agrees with this dire assessment. In a 2012 essay in the *New York Times*, he described coral reefs as "zombie ecosystems."

> **"The future is horrific. . . . There is no hope of reefs surviving to even mid-century in any form that we now recognize. If, and when, they go, they will take with them about one-third of the world's marine biodiversity. . . . This is the path of a mass extinction event."[5]**
>
> —*Charlie Veron, one of the world's foremost experts on coral reefs*

He states, "Overfishing, ocean acidification and pollution are pushing coral reefs into oblivion. Each of those forces alone is fully capable of causing the global collapse of coral reefs; together, they assure it."[6] Bradbury is especially upset that more scientists do not share his view. He points to the 2012 International Coral Reef Symposium, which produced a statement signed by 2,000 scientists and conservationists calling upon governments to save reefs. Bradbury feels these scientists should accept the fact that reefs will not survive. He says, "By persisting in the false belief that coral reefs have a future, we grossly misallocate the funds needed to cope with the fallout from their collapse."[7]

THE NON-DOOMSDAY EXPERTS

Others think reefs may not be completely doomed. John Bruno, a marine ecologist from the University of North Carolina, agrees that reefs have changed radically. In the Caribbean, he notes, coral populations have declined by at least 50 percent, and probably more than 75 percent.[8] But he does not think reefs will collapse in the next generation. The situation is complex and depends on many things, Bruno says—how soon greenhouse gas emissions are slowed, how

ACCELERATION AND INERTIA

Ecologist Roger Bradbury says coral reefs are doomed because the three factors causing their demise (ocean acidification, pollution, and overfishing) are governed by acceleration and inertia. Acidification and pollution are accelerating based on world economic growth, and they double in size approximately every two decades. They also show extreme inertia, an inability to change direction in less than 20 to 50 years. Thus, they are "unstoppable and irreversible." Studies at the University of British Columbia indicate that global fishing pressure continues to accelerate even as catches decline. Bradbury says, "This is not a story that gives me any pleasure to tell. But . . . it will be a disaster for the hundreds of millions of people in poor, tropical countries like Indonesia and the Philippines who depend on coral reefs for food. It will also threaten the tourism industry. . . . And, almost an afterthought, it will be a tragedy for global conservation as hot spots of biodiversity are destroyed."[9]

large human populations become, and whether people learn to manage fish populations intelligently. Although reefs are under pressure, Bruno does not think, like Bradbury, that these pressures are accelerating. He thinks reefs will persist in an altered and less biodiverse form. But, Bruno admits, "I have been called a pathological optimist."[10]

Andrew Revkin is a *New York Times* reporter and a senior fellow at the Pace Academy for Applied Environmental Studies. Revkin has seen and documented the degradation occurring on coral reefs, but he also sees hope. Reefs have a lot of resilience, he says. Pollution can be decreased, and MPAs can provide nursery areas to help repopulate the reefs. Although coral reefs as humans have known them are probably doomed, corals will survive and, in future millennia, will likely return to their full glory. Ecologist Carl Safina agrees. He points out that some corals are heat tolerant and some can survive relatively large pH swings. Thus, although the reefs we know today may not be here tomorrow, new reefs with different adaptations might be. Safina quotes the movie *Jurassic Park*: "Life finds a way."[11]

BRIGHT SPOTS IN REEF ECOSYSTEMS

In a survey of 6,000 reefs in 46 countries, researchers found 15 reefs they considered "bright spots." The reefs had more fish than expected, given they were exposed to stresses such as high human populations and poor environmental conditions. These were not necessarily pristine reefs, but local people were strongly involved in their management. The researchers hope these reefs will highlight good management methods that can be applied to other areas. The study also identified 35 "dark spots," or reefs with fewer fish than expected. On these reefs, people net fish intensively and keep freezers to stockpile fish for market.[12]

New research supports these assessments. A team of French researchers showed that, while some coral species have been declining for 30 years or more, other species

Lobe coral, *Porites lobata*, is widespread throughout the Indian and Pacific Oceans. It recovers more quickly from bleaching than many other species of coral.

are remaining stable or increasing, and some are even recovering. On the seven reefs studied, certain types of coral, such as *Porites*, actually overcome warming temperatures and increase in number. Corals most likely to survive are those with the highest heat tolerance, the highest population growth rates, or the greatest longevity. The question is, will the new coral reefs that flourish under climate change continue to meet the needs of human populations?

A WORLD WITHOUT CORAL REEFS

If the doomsayers are correct, today's reefs will be replaced by a slimy, algae-covered, hard ocean bottom, covered with limestone rubble. There will be algal and microbial photosynthesis, and many jellyfish grazing on microbes, but few fish. This transformation would have both direct and indirect effects on human life. According to a 2014 United Nations study, warming oceans and ocean acidification will cost the world economy more than $1 trillion by 2100—most of it due to loss of coral reefs.[13]

Up to one billion people depend on coral reefs for fish and other foods.[14] Their loss would be a disaster, especially for island nations such as Indonesia and the Philippines. Reefs also protect coastal communities. Their three-dimensional structure absorbs 80 to 90 percent of the energy from waves and storms.[15] Storm damage would be much greater without the buffering capacity of reefs. Reef biodiversity supports a huge tourism industry in developed countries such as the United States, Australia, and Japan. Reefs are a source of medicines to battle disease-causing bacteria and fungi. The drug AZT, used to treat HIV, comes from chemicals found in a Caribbean reef sponge, and some of the new research on cancer drugs is focusing on marine organisms.

Biodiversity of coral structures provides nursery habitats and hiding places for reef fish. Also, biodiversity provides a cushion of extra species to rebuild the reef community after catastrophes. In a diverse community, at least some species are likely to survive, providing the basis for a new (and perhaps different) reef community.

Many species will have trouble surviving the death of reef ecosystems.

If reefs die, these benefits will die with them. If reefs persist in some form, the situation will not be as dire. But even optimists expect problems. There will be a loss of food and building materials, of tourism income, and of personal and community protections. The stunning displays of living beauty treasured by tourists will be gone. Even those not economically affected will feel the loss.

SAVING WHAT'S LEFT

Coral reef scientists agree that if coral reefs are to be saved in any form, a major priority must be a quick decrease in carbon dioxide emissions to slow ocean warming and

CORAL REEF ETHICS

Professor Peter F. Sale sees little hope of coral reefs surviving, primarily because of climate change. Statistics show how dire the situation is: Coral growth rates on the GBR have declined 40 percent in the past 40 years due to ocean acidification. It would take more than 700 years to reverse ocean acidification, even if people began aggressively removing carbon dioxide from the ocean. But besides climate change, Sale says, more than 90 percent of the world's commercial fish biomass has been lost due to overfishing since the 1940s, coastal pollution is rising, and protected areas are not being protected. Sale sees this as a matter of ethics. "Knowing what we are doing, do we have the ethical right to eliminate an entire ecosystem from this planet?" he asks. "It's never been done before. But watching as our actions lead to the loss of all coral reefs on the planet is like removing all rainforests. I don't believe we have that right."[19]

acidification. Professor Peter F. Sale of the University of Windsor, Ontario, Canada, says, "Aiming for [carbon dioxide] at 350 [parts per million], or a total warming of around [1.8 degrees Fahrenheit (1°C)] is scientifically defendable, and would give reefs a good chance."[16] As of January 2017, global carbon dioxide levels were already at 405 parts per million.[17] World leaders had agreed to limit warming to 3.6 degrees Fahrenheit (2°C) by the end of the century.[18] Thus, based on Sale's estimates, the limits to warming agreed on by world leaders are too high to keep coral reefs safe, or even give them a chance to survive.

Others think something can be done about local threats to reefs. Reef expert Charles Sheppard notes that we cannot manage coral reefs, but we can manage human impacts on them—pollution, dredging, and overfishing. If these factors are managed so the reef is kept reasonably healthy, it will be more able to withstand climate change impacts. Sheppard says developers should be required to do environmental

Researchers drill core samples from coral in the Philippines to study how ocean changes are affecting its growth.

Both local and global action are likely necessary to preserve coral reefs' diversity.

assessments and follow their guidelines before any coastal construction project is allowed that might damage reefs by sedimentation or other pollution.

Finally, many see a great need for more MPAs, particularly those that allow no fishing or other human activity. They feel other areas should be set aside for fishing, but that, without completely protected areas to serve as refuges and nurseries, reef organisms have no hope of survival. Such refuges should be located as far from human settlements as possible.

Reef expert Richard Aronson of the Florida Institute of Technology is very concerned that people are taking an either-or approach to dealing with reef dangers. He says, "What's the point of [attacking local threats such as pollution] if coral reefs are doomed by climate change? It's a total waste of resources."[20] Instead, Aronson says, there must be simultaneous action on local and global threats. There must be decisive action to counter climate change and limit the rise of temperature and acidity on reefs. At the same time, local and regional managers must protect reefs from pollution, sedimentation, destructive fishing, and other hazards.

The evidence is strong that coral reef ecosystems are indeed collapsing because of an interacting web of threats. Rising temperatures, increasing acidification, overfishing, and various local threats are all combining to weaken and destroy coral reefs. Approximately one-fourth of Earth's coral reefs are already dead, and another one-half have been damaged to various degrees. Only one-fourth can be considered healthy, and only a tiny percentage still show the lush biodiversity they had only a few decades ago.[21] If reefs are to have any chance of surviving into the next century, all citizens—not just scientists and conservation managers—must recognize the dangers and do their part to preserve reefs. This might mean lobbying politicians and industries to decrease the input of greenhouse gases. It might mean decreasing your own personal input of greenhouse gases. It might mean refusing to buy reef fish to stock your aquarium, or refusing to buy reef-based souvenirs such as shells or coral jewelry. Every protective action, no matter how small, can help keep coral reefs alive for another day.

CAUSE AND EFFECT

Climate Change
→ Rising temperatures
→ Rising acidity

Pollution
→ Sediment
→ Excess nutrients
→ Toxins (pesticides, cyanide)

Fishing/Exploitation
→ Overfishing, aquarium harvest
→ Blast (dynamite) fishing
→ Mining for coral

Tourism → Coral damage, theft

98

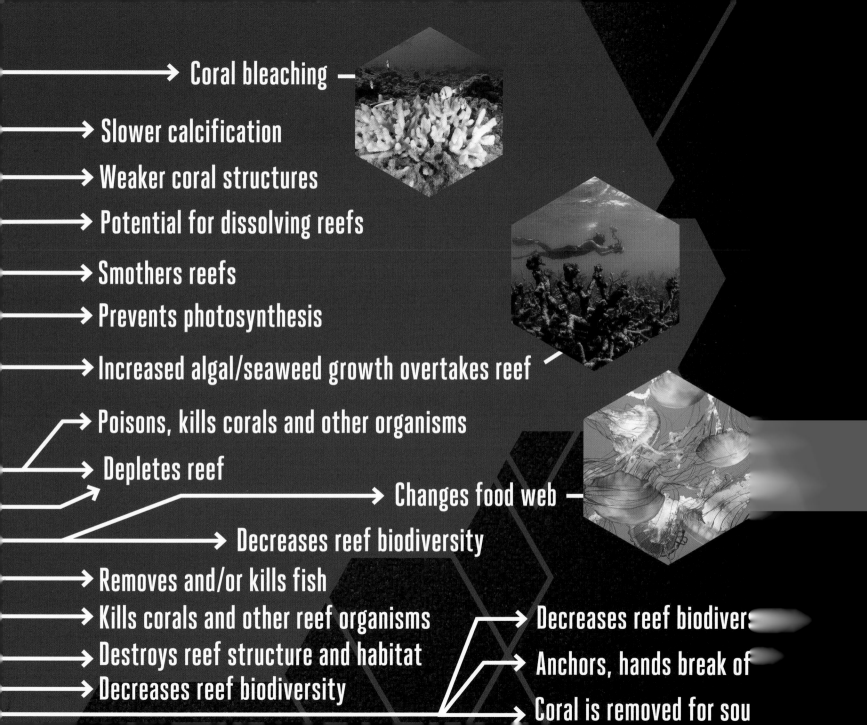

Coral bleaching

Slower calcification

Weaker coral structures

Potential for dissolving reefs

Smothers reefs

Prevents photosynthesis

Increased algal/seaweed growth overtakes reef

Poisons, kills corals and other organisms

Depletes reef

Changes food web

Decreases reef biodiversity

Removes and/or kills fish

Kills corals and other reef organisms

Destroys reef structure and habitat

Decreases reef biodiversity

Decreases reef biodiver

Anchors, hands break of

Coral is removed for sou

ESSENTIAL FACTS

WHAT IS HAPPENING

Coral reefs around the world are dying or are in poor health and in danger of death. Australia's Great Barrier Reef and reefs in the Caribbean are among the most endangered.

THE CAUSES

The most serious and damaging cause of reef decline is climate change, which results in higher temperatures and higher acidity on reefs. High temperatures cause coral bleaching, or death from the loss of the corals' symbiotic algae, zooxanthellae. Higher acidity makes it more difficult for corals to build skeletons and causes weaker skeletons. Many local stresses also contribute to reef damage and death. Some, such as sediment and nutrient enrichment, are from land-based activities. Others, including overfishing and removing corals from reefs, are direct attacks on the reef.

WHEN AND WHERE IT'S HAPPENING

Coral destruction is happening on coral reefs around the world. Climate change is a worldwide phenomenon, although the amount of change varies with location. The worst local stresses on corals occur in regions of high human population, such as the Caribbean and the Coral Triangle in the South Pacific.

KEY PLAYERS

People who dive on reefs, or buy aquarium fish captured on reefs, have a direct impact on coral reef health. The local fishers who live near, and depend on, reefs affect those reefs and have a stake in their survival. Recently, coral reef experts have begun to sound the alarm about the destruction of reefs and their likely death as an ecosystem by mid-century. These include Charlie Veron of the Australian Institute of Marine Science; ecologist Roger Bradbury of Australian National University; and professors Peter F. Sale of the University of Windsor, Ontario, and Charles Sheppard, University of Warwick, UK.

WHAT IT MEANS FOR THE FUTURE

Most experts expect that, by approximately 2050, coral reef ecosystems will either be extinct or very different. If they survive, reefs will be smaller and much less diverse. They will have a different mix of corals that better tolerate high temperature and acidity. In either case, the one billion people who depend on coral reefs for food and livelihoods will be in serious trouble. The tourism industry now dependent on coral reefs will be seriously damaged. Efforts are being made to preserve reefs in Marine Protected Areas and, in some cases, to rebuild them after destruction.

QUOTE

"The future is horrific. . . . There is no hope of reefs surviving even to mid-century in any form that we now recognize. If, and when, they go, they will take with them about one-third of the world's marine biodiversity. . . . This is the path of a mass extinction event."

—Charlie Veron, one of the world's foremost experts on coral reefs

GLOSSARY

barrier reef

A coral reef that runs mostly parallel to shore, separated from land by a lagoon.

calcification

The production of calcium carbonate by corals and other reef animals to produce hard skeletons and shells.

cay

A sand-covered island with coral as a base.

dredge

To dig or deepen a waterway by removing earth from the body of water's bottom.

ecosystem service

A benefit people receive from natural ecosystems, including provisioning services such as food and water, regulating services such as flood control, cultural services such as recreation, and supporting services such as nutrient cycling or pollination.

greenhouse gas

A gas that absorbs infrared radiation and traps heat in the atmosphere.

pH

The measure of how acidic a mixture is.

photosynthesis

The process used by plants and other organisms to convert sunlight into usable energy.

phylum

In biology, a large category of related organisms. For example, the phylum porifera includes sponges and the phylum arthropoda includes organisms with exoskeletons and segmented bodies.

phytoplankton

Microscopic marine plants.

polyp

A tiny animal with a cylindrical body and mouth surrounded by tentacles.

precipitate

To separate out from a mixture.

quota

The number or share given to each participant.

rebar

A reinforcing steel bar used to strengthen concrete.

salinity

The concentration of salts in the water.

thermocline

Layer of ocean where the temperature changes very rapidly; separates the surface layer from the deep ocean.

trawl

To fish with a large net dragged along the sea bottom.

zooplankton

Microscopic marine animals.

ADDITIONAL RESOURCES

SELECTED BIBLIOGRAPHY

"Coral Reef Ecology." *Coral Reefs 101*. Coral Reef Alliance, 2014. Web. 27 Jan. 2017.

Rohwer, Forest, and Merry Youle. *Coral Reefs in the Microbial Seas*. United States: Plaid, 2010. Print.

Sheppard, Charles. *Coral Reefs: A Very Short Introduction*. Oxford, UK: Oxford UP, 2014. Print.

FURTHER READINGS

Knowlton, Nancy. *Citizens of the Sea: Wondrous Creatures from the Census of Marine Life*. Washington, DC: National Geographic, 2010. Print.

Sheppard, Anne. *Coral Reefs: Secret Cities of the Sea*. London: Natural History Museum, 2015. Print.

Wicks, Maris. *Science Comics: Coral Reefs: Cities of the Ocean*. New York: First Second, 2016. Print.

WEBSITES

To learn more about Ecological Disasters, visit **abdobooklinks.com**. These links are routinely monitored and updated to provide the most current information available.

FOR MORE INFORMATION

For more information on this subject, contact or visit the following organizations:

Coral Reef Alliance

1330 Broadway, Suite 1602
Oakland, CA 94612
1-888-Coral-Reef
http://coral.org/what-we-do/reduce-local-reef-threats/

The Coral Reef Alliance website includes Coral Reefs 101, a short course on coral reefs and threats facing them. The alliance runs many programs to benefit coral reefs, working closely with the communities who depend on reefs, and the website offers ways for interested people to volunteer or help.

Reef Environmental Education Foundation (REEF)

P.O. Box 370246
98300 Overseas Hwy
Key Largo, FL 33037
305-852-0030
http://www.reef.org/

REEF is a conservation organization that educates and enlists divers and other marine enthusiasts to help preserve oceans and reefs. They have educational programs, citizen scientist projects such as fish surveys, internships, and REEF trips. All are described on their website.

SOURCE NOTES

CHAPTER 1. THE GREAT BARRIER REEF

1. "Facts About the Great Barrier Reef." *Australian Government: Great Barrier Reef Marine Park Authority.* Commonwealth of Australia, 2016. Web. 27 Jan. 2017.

2. Biodiversity and Climate Change Expert Advisory Group. "Fact Sheet: The Great Barrier Reef and Climate Change." *Australia's Biodiversity and Climate Change—A Strategic Assessment of the Vulnerability of Australia's Biodiversity to Climate Change.* 2013. PDF. 27 Jan. 2017.

3. Michael Greshko. "Warming Threatens the Great Barrier Reef Even More Than We Thought." *National Geographic.* National Geographic, 14 Apr. 2016. Web. 27 Jan. 2017.

4. "Facts About the Great Barrier Reef." *Australian Government: Great Barrier Reef Marine Park Authority.* Commonwealth of Australia, 2016. Web. 27 Jan. 2017.

5. Ibid.

6. "The Great Barrier Reef, Queensland—World Heritage Values." *Australian Government: Department of the Environment and Energy.* Commonwealth of Australia, n.d. Web. 27 Jan. 2017.

7. Biodiversity and Climate Change Expert Advisory Group. "Fact Sheet: The Great Barrier Reef and Climate Change." *Australian Government: Department of the Environment and Energy.* Commonwealth of Australia, 2013. PDF. 27 Jan. 2017.

8. Euan McKirdy. "Study: Over 90% of Great Barrier Reef Suffering from Bleaching." *CNN.* CNN, 20 Apr. 2016. Web. 27 Jan. 2017.

9. Michael Greshko. "Warming Threatens the Great Barrier Reef Even More Than We Thought." *National Geographic.* National Geographic Society, 14 Apr. 2016. Web. 27 Jan. 2017.

10. Michael Slezak. "The Great Barrier Reef: A Catastrophe Laid Bare." *Guardian.* Guardian, 6 June 2016. Web. 27 Jan. 2017.

11. John Upton. "Bleak Picture of Great Barrier Reef's Changing Chemistry." *Climate Central.* Climate Central, 23 Feb. 2016. Web. 27 Jan. 2017.

CHAPTER 2. WHAT IS A CORAL REEF?

1. "Announcing the Release of the World Atlas of Coral Reefs." *Coral Reef Unit.* United Nations Environment Programme, 3 June 2013. Web. 27 Jan. 2017.

2. "Oil and Coral: General Coral Reef Facts." *NOAA Fisheries Southeast Regional Office.* National Oceanic and Atmospheric Administration, n.d. Web. 27 Jan. 2017.

3. "Corals: Zooxanthellae . . . What's That?" *NOAA Ocean Service Education.* National Oceanic and Atmospheric Administration, 25 Mar. 2008. Web. 27 Jan. 2017.

4. "Corals Without Sunlight?" *Ocean Portal.* Smithsonian National Museum of Natural History, 2016. 27 Jan. 2017.

5. David Maxwell Braun. "Coral Reefs Provide Services Worth $172 Billion to Humans Every Year." *National Geographic.* National Geographic, 16 Oct. 2009. Web. 27 Jan. 2017.

6. "Coral: Anthozoa." *National Geographic.* National Geographic, n.d. Web. 27 Jan. 2017.

7. Richard Aronson. Personal communication. 9 Nov. 2016.

8. "Coral Reef Ecology: How Coral Reefs Grow." *Coral Reefs 101.* Coral Reef Alliance, 2014. Web. 27 Jan. 2017.

CHAPTER 3. HOW ARE OCEANS CHANGING?

1. John Cook. "Are CO2 Levels Increasing?" *Skeptical Science.* John Cook, 2016. Web. 27 Jan. 2017.

2. "Climate Change Indicators: Ocean Heat." *US Environmental Protection Agency.* EPA, 11 Aug. 2016. Web. 27 Jan. 2017.

3. NASA. "Graphic: The Relentless Rise of Carbon Dioxide." *Global Climate Change.* NASA, 15 Sept. 2016. Web. 27 Jan. 2017.

4. "Sea Level Rise." *National Geographic Reference.* National Geographic, n.d. Web. 27 Jan. 2017.

5. Brady Dennis and Chris Mooney. "Scientists Nearly Double Sea Level Rise Projections for 2200, Because of Antarctica." *Washington Post.* Washington Post, 30 Mar. 2016. Web. 27 Jan. 2017.

6. "Climate Change Indicators: Ocean Acidity." *US Environmental Protection Agency*. EPA, Aug. 2016. 27 Jan. 2017.

7. Oliver Milman. "Soaring Ocean Temperature Is 'Greatest Hidden Challenge of Our Generation.'" *Guardian*. Guardian, 5 Sept. 2016. Web. 27 Jan. 2017.

8. Holli Riebeek. "The Ocean's Carbon Balance." *Earth Observatory*. NASA, 30 June 2008. Web. 27 Jan. 2017.

9. "Marine Problems: Pollution." *WWF*. WWF, 2017. Web. 27 Jan. 2017.

CHAPTER 4. HOW DO RISING TEMPERATURES AFFECT CORAL REEFS?

1. Tundi Agardy. "America's Coral Reefs: Awash with Problems." *Issues in Science and Technology*, 20.2 (Winter 2004): n.pag. Web. 27 Jan. 2017.

2. John Cook. "How Global Warming Is Driving Mass Coral Bleaching." *Skeptical Science*. John Cook, 24 Apr. 2016. Web. 27 Jan. 2017.

3. Chelsea Harvey. "Why Dead Coral Reefs Could Mark the Beginning of 'Dangerous' Climate Change." *Washington Post*. Washington Post, 12 Apr. 2016. Web. 27 Jan. 2017.

4. "Coral Bleaching and Ocean Acidification Are Two Climate-Related Impacts to Coral Reefs." *Florida Keys National Marine Sanctuary*. NOAA, 8 Dec. 2011. Web. 27 Jan. 2017.

5. Ove Hoegh-Guldberg and Janice Lough, Expert Reviewers. "Climate Change and Coral Bleaching." *Nova*. Australian Academy of Science, 14 May 2015. Web. 27 Jan. 2017.

6. Chelsea Harvey. "Why Dead Coral Reefs Could Mark the Beginning of 'Dangerous' Climate Change." *Washington Post*. Washington Post, 12 Apr. 2016. Web. 27 Jan. 2017.

7. Adam Vaughan. "Scientists Reveal Which Coral Reefs Can Survive Global Warming." *Guardian*. Guardian, 14 Jan. 2015. Web. 27 Jan. 2017.

8. Chelsea Harvey. "Why Dead Coral Reefs Could Mark the Beginning of 'Dangerous' Climate Change." *Washington Post*. Washington Post, 12 Apr. 2016. Web. 27 Jan. 2017.

9. Ibid.

10. Ibid.

CHAPTER 5. A HOT ACID BATH

1. Rob Monroe. "How Much CO2 Can the Oceans Take Up?" *The Keeling Curve*. Scripps Institution of Oceanography, 3 July 2013. Web. 27 Jan. 2017.

2. "Ocean Acidification." *Ocean Portal*. Smithsonian National Museum of Natural History, 2016. Web. 27 Jan. 2017.

3. Ibid.

4. "Ocean Acidification." *Pristine Seas*. National Geographic, n.d. Web. 27 Jan. 2017.

5. Forest Rohwer and Merry Youle. *Coral Reefs in the Microbial Seas*. United States: Plaid, 2010. Print. 49–50.

6. Hanover Matz. "Coral Reefs and the Threat of Ocean Acidification." *University of Miami Shark Research*. University of Miami, 17 Jan. 2014. Web. 27 Jan. 2017.

7. "Ocean Acidification." *Ocean Portal*. Smithsonian National Museum of Natural History, 2016. Web. 27 Jan. 2017.

8. Marcia Creary. "Impacts of Climate Change on Coral Reefs and the Marine Environment." *UN Chronicle*. United Nations, Apr. 2013. Web. 27 Jan. 2017.

9. Roger Bradbury. "A World without Coral Reefs." *New York Times*. New York Times, 13 July 2012. Web. 27 Jan. 2017.

CHAPTER 6. THREATS FROM OCEAN POLLUTION AND DISEASE

1. "How Pollution Affects Coral Reefs." *NOAA Celebrates 200 Years.* National Oceanic and Atmospheric Administration, 19 July 2012. Web. 27 Jan. 2017.

2. Charles Sheppard. *Coral Reefs: A Very Short Introduction.* Oxford, UK: Oxford UP, 2014. Print. 84.

3. Chantale Bégin, et al. "Effects of Protection and Sediment Stress on Coral Reefs in Saint Lucia." *PLoS One.* PLoS, 4 Feb. 2016. Web. 27 Jan. 2017.

4. Forest Rohwer and Merry Youle. *Coral Reefs in the Microbial Seas.* United States: Plaid, 2010. Print. 77.

5. "The Great Pacific Garbage Patch." *Crochet Coral Reef.* Institute for Figuring, n.d. Web. 27 Jan. 2017.

6. Ibid.

7. Ibid.

8. Angus Chen. "Here's How Much Plastic Enters the Ocean Each Year." *Science.* American Association for the Advancement of Science, 12 Feb. 2015. Web. 27 Jan. 2017.

CHAPTER 7. OVERFISHING AND TOURISM

1. Carl Safina and Erica Cirino. "So You Live Near a Coral Reef: Why Experts Say That's Not Good News for Reef Conservation." *Ocean Views.* National Geographic, 6 Apr. 2016. Web. 27 Jan. 2017.

2. Peter J. Mumby, et al. Chapter 4. Coral Reef Fisheries Management. *Towards Reef Resilience and Sustainable Livelihoods. A Handbook for Caribbean Coral Reef Managers.* Exeter, UK: U of Exeter. *Marine Spatial Ecology Lab.* Web. 27 Jan. 2017.

3. "Causes and Effects of Coastal Degradation." *WWF.* WWF, 2017. Web. 27 Jan. 2017.

4. Ibid.

5. "Coral Reefs and Exploitive Fishing." *Issue Briefs.* Coral Reef Alliance, 2014. Web. 27 Jan. 2017.

6. Jani Actman. "In Tanzania, a Horrific Fishing Tactic Destroys All Sea Life." *National Geographic.* National Geographic, 30 Dec. 2015. Web. 27 Jan. 2017.

7. "Status of and Threat to Coral Reefs." *International Coral Reef Initiative.* ICRI, n.d. Web. 27 Jan. 2017.

8. "Coral Reef Wildlife Trafficking for the Aquarium Trade." *Sea Shepherd.* Sea Shepherd, n.d. Web. 27 Jan. 2017.

9. Ibid.

10. "Threats to Coral Reefs—Human Impacts." *Mamanuca Environment Society.* Mamunuca Environment Society, n.d. Web. 27 Jan. 2017.

11. Roddy Scheer and Doug Moss. "How Dangerous Is It to Use Cyanide to Catch Fish?" *Earth Talk.* Scientific American, n.d. Web. 27 Jan. 2017.

CHAPTER 8. REEF CONSERVATION AND MANAGEMENT

1. Brian Records. "What I Learned Restoring the World's Largest Coral Reef with Mars." *GreenBiz.* GreenBiz, 13 Nov. 2015. Web. 27 Jan. 2017.

2. "Coral Reefs." *National Fisheries and Wildlife Foundation.* NFWF, 2016. Web. 27 Jan. 2017.

3. Carl Safina and Erica Cirino. "So You Live Near a Coral Reef: Why Experts Say That's Not Good News for Reef Conservation." *Ocean Views.* National Geographic, 6 Apr. 2016. Web. 27 Jan. 2017.

4. Laura E. Dee, Stephanie S. Horii, and Daniel J. Thornhill. "Conservation and Management of Ornamental Coral Reef Wildlife: Successes, Shortcomings, and Future Directions." *Biological Conservation* 169 (Jan. 2014): 225–237. *ScienceDirect.* Web. 27 Jan. 2017.

5. "Global Facts about MPAs and Marine Reserves." *Protect Planet Ocean.* Protect Planet Ocean, 2010. Web. 27 Jan. 2017.

6. "What Is a Marine Protected Area?" *National Ocean Service.* NOAA, 28 Sept. 2016. Web. 27 Jan. 2017.

7. Jane J. Lee. "The Pacific Is About to Get a Massive New Ocean Reserve." *National Geographic*. National Geographic, 22 Oct. 2015. Web. 27 Jan. 2017.

8. Jane J. Lee. "Chile Creates Largest Marine Reserve in the Americas." *National Geographic*. National Geographic, 5 Oct. 2015. Web. 27 Jan. 2017.

9. Brian Clark Howard. "World's Largest Single Marine Reserve Created in Pacific." *National Geographic.* National Geographic, 18 Mar. 2015. Web. 27 Jan. 2017.

10. Cynthia Barnett. "Hawaii Is Now Home to an Ocean Reserve Twice the Size of Texas." *National Geographic*. National Geographic, 26 Aug. 2016. Web. 27 Jan. 2017.

CHAPTER 9. ARE CORAL REEFS DOOMED?

1. David Adam. "How Global Warming Sealed the Fate of the World's Coral Reefs." *Guardian*. Guardian, 2 Sept. 2009. Web. 27 Jan. 2017.

2. Ibid.

3. Ibid.

4. Ibid.

5. Ibid.

6. Roger Bradbury. "A World without Coral Reefs." *New York Times*. New York Times, 13 July 2012. Web. 27 Jan. 2017.

7. Ibid

8. Andrew C. Revkin. "Reefs in the Anthropocene—Zombie Ecology?" *New York Times*. New York Times, 14 July 2012. Web. 27 Jan. 2017.

9. Roger Bradbury. "A World without Coral Reefs." *New York Times*. New York Times, 13 July 2012. Web. 27 Jan. 2017.

10. Andrew C. Revkin. "Reefs in the Anthropocene—Zombie Ecology?" *New York Times*. New York Times, 14 July 2012. Web. 27 Jan. 2017.

11. Ibid.

12. "Bright Spots Shine Light on the Future of Coral Reefs." *Phys. org.* Phys.org, 15 June 2016. Web. 27 Jan. 2017.

13. Brian Stallard. "Are Coral Reefs Doomed? Changing? Ignored? What We Know So Far." *Nature World News*. Nature World News, 23 Aug. 2015. Web. 27 Jan. 2017.

14. Jessica Carilli. "Why Are Coral Reefs Important?" *Scitable: Saltwater Science*. NatureEducation, 17 June 2013. Web. 27 Jan. 2017.

15. Ibid.

16. Hannah Osborne. "World's Coral Reefs Doomed Even If COP21 Is 'Wildly Successful' Expert Says." *International Business Times*. IBTimes, 16 Aug. 2015. Web. 27 Jan. 2017.

17. "The Keeling Curve." *The Keeling Curve*. Scripps Institution of Oceanography, 23 Jan. 2017. Web. 27 Jan. 2017.

18. Hannah Osborne. "World's Coral Reefs Doomed Even If COP21 Is 'Wildly Successful' Expert Says." *International Business Times*. IBTimes, 16 Aug. 2015. Web. 27 Jan. 2017.

19. Ibid.

20. Richard Aronson. Personal communication. 9 Nov. 2016.

21. Charles Sheppard. *Coral Reefs: A Very Short Introduction*. Oxford, UK: Oxford UP, 2014. Print. 104.

INDEX

ABOUT THE AUTHOR

Carol Hand has a PhD in zoology with a specialization in marine ecology and a special interest in environmental and climate science. Her PhD dissertation was on coral reef fisheries. Before becoming a science writer, she taught college, wrote for standardized-testing companies, and developed multimedia science curricula. She has written more than 30 books for young people, including many on science and environmental topics.